Angelina Jolie

Angelina Jolie

people in the NEWS

Angelina Jolie

by Rachel Lynette

LUCENT BOOKS

An imprint of Thomson Gale, a part of The Thomson Corporation

THOMSON

™

GALE

Detroit • New York • San Francisco • San Diego • New Haven, Conn.
Waterville, Maine • London • Munich

THOMSON
━━━━━✦━━━━━ ™
GALE

To Lucy—may you also be bold, brave and free

LIBRARY OF CONGRESS CATALOGING-IN-PUBLICATION DATA

Lynette, Rachel.
Angelina Jolie / by Rachel Lynette.
    p. cm. — (People in the news)
Includes bibliographical references and index.
ISBN 1-59018-973-6 (hardcover : alk. paper)
1. Jolie, Angelina, 1975——Juvenile literature. 2. Motion picture actors and actresses—United States—Biography—Juvenile literature. I. Title.
II. Series: People in the news (San Diego, Calif.)
PN2287.J583L96 2007
791.4302'8092—dc22
[B]
                                                        2006017111

Printed in the United States of America

Contents

ame and celebrity are alluring. People are drawn to those who walk in fame's spotlight, whether they are known for great accomplishments or for notorious deeds. The lives of the famous pique public interest and attract attention, perhaps because their experiences seem in some ways so different from, yet in other ways so similar to, our own.

Newspapers, magazines, and television regularly capitalize on this fascination with celebrity by running profiles of famous people. For example, television programs such as *Entertainment Tonight* devote all of their programming to stories about entertainment and entertainers. Magazines such as *People* fill their pages with stories of the private lives of famous people. Even newspapers, newsmagazines, and television news frequently delve into the lives of well-known personalities. Despite the number of articles and programs, few provide more than a superficial glimpse at their subjects.

Lucent's People in the News series offers young readers a deeper look into the lives of today's newsmakers, the influences that have shaped them, and the impact they have had in their fields of endeavor and on other people's lives. The subjects of the series hail from many disciplines and walks of life. They include authors, musicians, athletes, political leaders, entertainers, entrepreneurs, and others who have made a mark on modern life and who, in many cases, will continue to do so for years to come.

These biographies are more than factual chronicles. Each book emphasizes the contributions, accomplishments, or deeds that have brought fame or notoriety to the individual and shows how that person has influenced modern life. Authors portray their subjects in a realistic, unsentimental light. For example, Bill Gates—the cofounder and chief executive officer of the software giant Microsoft—has been instrumental in making personal computers the most vital tool of the modern age. Few dispute his business savvy, his perseverance, or his technical expertise, yet critics say he is ruthless in his dealings with competitors and driven more by his desire to maintain Microsoft's dominance in the computer industry than by an interest in furthering technology.

In these books, young readers will encounter inspiring stories about real people who achieved success despite enormous obstacles. Oprah Winfrey—the most powerful, most watched, and wealthiest woman on television today—spent the first six years of her life in the care of her grandparents while her unwed mother sought work and a better life elsewhere. Her adolescence was colored by promiscuity, pregnancy at age fourteen, rape, and sexual abuse.

Each author documents and supports his or her work with an array of primary and secondary source quotations taken from diaries, letters, speeches, and interviews. All quotes are footnoted to show readers exactly how and where biographers derive their information and provide guidance for further research. The quotations enliven the text by giving readers eyewitness views of the life and accomplishments of each person covered in the People in the News series.

In addition, each book in the series includes photographs, annotated bibliographies, timelines, and comprehensive indexes. For both the casual reader and the student researcher, the People in the News series offers insight into the lives of today's newsmakers—people who shape the way we live, work, and play in the modern age.

Exceptional Angelina

"Be brave, be bold, be free."[1] These words of advice were given to Angelina Jolie by her mother, and Jolie's life is proof that she took them to heart. Jolie lives with abandon, often daring to say and do things that others would not. Unlike other celebrities, she has not employed a publicist during most of her career, so for many years, no one told her what to say—or what not to. Her often controversial choices and her outspoken honesty about her own life have made her one of the most talked about celebrities of her generation. She speaks openly about periods when she has felt depressed and suicidal, her lifelong fascination with knives, her uninhibited sexuality, her many tattoos, and her intense feelings about the people she loves. Jolie has been accused of doing outrageous things only to garner media attention, but for the most part, she does not care what other people think of her. She has said that she is simply living her life and does not understand what all the fuss is about.

From the moment she was born, Jolie was no stranger to Hollywood, thanks to her famous father, Jon Voight. Her parents divorced when she was a toddler, and her childhood was a turbulent mix of living in near obscurity with her mother and mixing with the elite of Hollywood with her dad. Jolie found success early, in part because of her exotic beauty and smoldering sexuality. She did not shy away from nudity in her movies, and many of her early roles took advantage of her willingness to appear in sexy outfits—or even nothing at all. However, it soon became obvious that there was more to Jolie than her stunning beauty; she was also a gifted actor.

Jolie devotes herself to the roles she plays, often blurring the lines between her own personality and that of the character she is portraying. She does not just act a part; in many ways, she becomes it. For several years, Jolie felt that she did not have a life of her own, but rather lived through her characters. Although exhausting for Jolie, this acting method resulted in several critically acclaimed performances. In 2000, her talent was recognized with a Best Supporting Actress Oscar for her role as Lisa in *Girl, Interrupted*. Since then, she has starred in over a dozen movies, including the big-budget action-thriller *Lara Croft: Tomb Raider*.

Like many of her movies, *Tomb Raider* had a disappointing show at the box office. Yet despite the fact that Jolie has a knack for choosing mediocre and sometimes even appallingly bad movies, she is still one of the highest-paid and most sought-after stars in Hollywood, commanding a salary of well over $10 million per picture. Directors admire her talent and appreciate her no-nonsense work ethic and commitment to her roles. Fans

The film industry recognized Angelina Jolie's talent by awarding her an Oscar for her portrayal of Lisa (right) in **Girl, Interrupted.**

Jolie meets with Sudanese refugees in 2004 in her role as a United Nations goodwill ambassador.

continue to be drawn to her charismatic beauty and intrigued with her personal life.

Jolie takes her relationships with the people that she loves as seriously as she takes her acting. Although she is estranged from her father, she has an unusually close relationship with her brother. The tabloids have paired her with nearly every male actor she has worked with, although she has rarely engaged in casual relationships with her colleagues. When Jolie did find love with actor Billy Bob Thornton, she was open with the media about the eccentricities of their short but passionate marriage. While she was married to Thornton, Jolie adopted Maddox, an orphan from Cambodia. She devoted herself to motherhood, forgoing the services of a nanny and taking Maddox, and later her adopted daughter, Zahara, along whenever she traveled. Perhaps her most controversial relationship is her romance with actor Brad Pitt, who left his wife, actor Jennifer Aniston, to be with Jolie. Jolie and Pitt admitted to being romantically involved only after her swelling waistline made it clear that she was pregnant.

Although Jolie is known primarily for her career as an actor and her very public romantic relationships, she would rather people identify her with what she considers to be her real purpose in life: her work with the Office of the United Nations High Commissioner on Refugees (UNHCR). Jolie's interest in refugees began when she was filming *Lara Croft: Tomb Raider* on location in Cambodia. In August 2001, Jolie became a goodwill ambassador for the UNHCR. Jolie devoted herself to the work of the UNHCR with the same intensity that she had previously put into her movie roles. A great deal of her time and a sizable chunk of her income go to help refugees around the world. Jolie has said that she feels a greater sense of purpose working in the field than she ever has on a movie set. Eventually, she would like to quit making movies altogether in order to focus on her work with refugees and on her family.

Now in her thirties, Jolie feels that she has found a sense of stability and purpose that was lacking in her younger days. Her transformation from Hollywood bad girl to devoted mother and humanitarian has been a dramatic and positive change in her own life and has been held up as an example of how a Hollywood celebrity can make a real difference in the world. Jolie has no regrets about the choices she has made and the life she has lived. Instead, she is focused on her future, balancing her family life, her thriving career as an actor, and her active role in the UNHCR.

Chapter 1

Wild Child

Angelina Jolie Voight was born into a famous family on June 4, 1975, in Los Angeles. Her father was leading actor Jon Voight, and her mother, Marcheline Bertrand, also had acting ambitions before her marriage. Angelina Jolie was Bertrand and Voight's second child; their son, James Haven, was born two years earlier. By the time Jolie was born, Bertrand and Voight were unhappy with each other, and their marriage was in serious jeopardy.

Jolie's parents had married in 1971, when Bertrand was twenty and Voight was thirty-two and already a movie star. Many sources have reported that Voight was an unfaithful husband, and Voight himself has confessed to falling in love with another woman while married to Bertrand. When Jolie was just a year old, her father moved out, and the couple divorced in 1978, when Jolie was three.

Jon Voight was considered by many critics to be one of the most promising talents in Hollywood when he and Bertrand divorced. He had starred in several acclaimed movies, including *Midnight Cowboy* in 1969, for which he received an Oscar nomination; *Catch 22* in 1970; and *Deliverance* in 1972. In 1979, Voight won the Best Actor Oscar for his role as the paraplegic Vietnam veteran Luke Martin in *Coming Home*. Voight took acting seriously and committed himself to taking only roles that he considered to be meaningful and socially responsible. This decision meant that he turned down many parts that did not live up to his qualifications, and as a result he worked sporadically throughout most of Jolie's childhood.

Jolie shares a rare joyful moment with her father, Jon Voight, also an Oscar-winning actor.

Jolie's mother, Marcheline Bertrand, also had a background in drama. She grew up in Chicago and went on to study acting at the prestigious Lee Strasberg Theatre Institute. She gave up her dreams of becoming a professional actor, however, in order to raise her children. Not much is known about Bertrand's life, because she keeps a low profile and refuses to do interviews. Her friends describe her as a kind and giving person who is devoted to her children.

The divorce was hard on Bertrand, who was granted custody of the children. Jolie remembers her mother feeling stressed a lot of the time and crying frequently, and she recalls that although

Jolie's mother, Marcheline Bertrand (left), gave up hopes of an acting career to raise her family.

her parents remained friends, they often had arguments. The family's finances also contributed to the high degree of stress. Bertrand was monetarily dependent on Voight, and although he was a respected actor, the family was still not wealthy by Hollywood standards. Moreover, Voight gave away a great deal of money to various charities in which he was involved. According to Jolie, "My father was very uncomfortable about success. Like somehow it was great to live without, to give away everything you had. You know, to have money meant that maybe you were a bad person or something."[2] Jolie has said that although the family was financially secure, Bertrand could not afford to buy a house, so she and her children lived in a series of apartments.

Family Ties

Jolie's relationship with her father has been a rocky one. Both she and Voight are very independent and strong willed, which has often resulted in conflict. "He wasn't like a dad," she said. "He was this man I knew. He was a very complicated man and he always meant well and I always wanted to love him. But we both attacked each other because we both thought we were right about everything." The divorce added even more tension to their relationship, and Jolie felt her father's absence throughout her childhood. She says, "He wasn't there a lot, so I became strong for my mom."[3]

Jolie was much closer to her mother than to her father. Today, she admires her mother for sacrificing her dream of becoming an actor to focus on her children. Jolie says that even when she was growing up, their relationship was more like that of girlfriends than that of a parent and child. "My mom and I have always been close," said Jolie. "People don't know that because they're always writing about my father. She's a great lady. Catholic schoolgirl. Very sweet."[4]

Jolie also shared a special bond with her brother, James Haven. Throughout her often chaotic childhood, Jolie looked to him for stability and support. Haven was always there to comfort her and to reassure her that everything was going to be okay. "Both of us were quite young, and coming from a divorced family, we got very close," says Haven. "You need a certain support, and we gave that to each other."[5]

The Early Years

Jolie spent her earliest years with her mother and her brother, and her memories are mainly happy ones. She enjoyed playing dress up and describes herself as being very girlish, complete with curled hair and lipstick. "I used to wear costumes all the time," she says. "I had this black velvet frilly little showgirl thing with sparkles on my butt and I used to love those plastic high heels."[6] When she was in kindergarten, Jolie was part of a group called the Kissy Girls, who chased boys around the playground trying to kiss them. Jolie also remembers that some of the boys did not run. Two boys in particular got so much attention from Jolie that the school had to call her mother. But young Jolie's true love was Mr. Spock, the pointy-eared Vulcan from the original *Star Trek* TV show, who she says was her first girlhood crush.

Jolie was an outgoing child who loved to entertain people. Her father remembers her brother pointing the video camera at her when she was just a toddler, saying "Angie, act!"[7] and she would perform on cue. Sometimes Voight filmed his daughter and her friends, letting them pretend to audition for movie roles. Jolie made her real movie debut in 1982 at the age of seven, with a small part in *Lookin' to Get Out*, a film that her father both starred in and cowrote. Jolie played Tosh, the daughter of a gambler, who was played by her father.

Always Moving

The next few years were unsettling for Jolie. When she was eight, her mother moved the family across the country to Sneden's Landing in upstate New York. But the family did not stay there very long. Bertrand moved the family frequently. This was hard on her daughter, who says she longed for stability and a feeling of home:

Pictured here in her first movie role at age seven, Jolie acted alongside her father (right).

I never had a house growing up, I never had one home, I never had an attic that had old stuff in it. We always moved, lived in a lot of different apartments and nobody ever owned anything, so I was never rooted anywhere. And I always really dreamed of having that attic of things that I could go back up and look at, or just anything really—marks on the walls.[8]

Jolie has speculated that this lack of stability during this time in her life created a desire for tradition and roots, which manifested itself in an unusual interest in death and funerals. When she was nine, Jolie attended her grandfather's funeral. She was intrigued by the traditional aspects of the funeral service, and she liked the way the ceremony brought people together. For several years, Jolie's future career goal was to become a funeral director. She even ordered a handbook from the Funeral Service Institute, which she studied diligently.

Jon Voight

ngelina Jolie's handsome and talented father was one of the most promising young actors of the 1970s. But Voight wanted to be more than an actor. It was also important to him to help other people. He has committed to many charitable causes, and at different times in his life he has worked to help drug addicts, the homeless, farmers, Vietnam veterans, and the elderly. He also became involved in helping thousands of children in the USSR who were poisoned by radiation when the Chernobyl nuclear reactor exploded in 1986. Voight has been especially drawn to projects involving children.

His charity work, along with his commitment to do only serious roles, resulted in Voight acting in only six movies in the 1980s. Although he was often admired for his integrity and generosity, his choices took a toll on his children, who remember a childhood with financial difficulties and an often absent father.

Voight made a comeback in the 1990s, starring in many movies, including *Mission: Impossible* with Tom Cruise, *Anaconda* with Jennifer Lopez, and *Enemy of the State* with Will Smith. He has been working steadily ever since and remains one of Hollywood's most respected actors.

Actor Jon Voight rose to prominence in the 1970s.

Jolie also developed what would become a lifelong fascination with knives around this time. She often went to Renaissance fairs with her mother, where they immersed themselves in the customs, costumes, arts, and crafts of Europe in the fifteenth and sixteenth centuries. Jolie was drawn to the many weapons that were on display. She was especially interested in the roles that knives have played in history and in the traditions associated with them. She began collecting different kinds of knives from all over the world.

Back to Los Angeles

Jolie's mother moved the family back to California when her daughter was eleven years old. This allowed the children to see their father more often. In 1986, Jolie attended the Academy Awards with Voight, who had received a Best Actor nomination for his role in *Runaway Train*. A picture of her at the ceremony later appeared in *Jane* magazine. According to *Rolling Stone* reporter Mim Udovitch, she was "all mouth and eyes and Eighties hair, decked out in enough pearls and white lace for an entire congregation's worth of brides at a Tom Thumb wedding."[9] Jolie said that the experience made her feel like an imposter because instead of just being herself, she had tried to look like the other women at the ceremony. In addition, she found the ceremony boring.

Although her experience at the awards was less than inspirational, by thirteen, Jolie had decided that she wanted to be an actor. Her parents encouraged her to learn the craft. As her mother had been, she was accepted into the Lee Strasberg Theatre Institute. At the institute, which she attended for two years, she learned the Method acting technique and appeared in several stage productions.

Misfit

Jolie also went to Beverly Hills High School, where she felt she did not fit in with her classmates, most of whom came from wealthy Hollywood families. Although most people assumed that her family was well-off, this was not the case. According to Jolie, "My dad was sort of 'out of Hollywood' when I was growing up. People thought we had a big house, but we rented an apartment, like Slums of Beverly Hills."[10] Rather than buying expensive clothes at upscale boutiques on Rodeo Drive like many of her classmates, Jolie purchased most of hers from thrift shops.

By the time she was fourteen, Jolie was feeling depressed a great deal of the time. According to *Rolling Stone* magazine, she did not like school, where her already-restless nature made it hard for her to sit through classes in which she had little interest. While the teachers droned on, Jolie's thoughts turned to knives and death. She showed *Rolling Stone* reporter Chris Heath one of her school notebooks, which was filled with drawings of swords and daggers and definitions such as "Death: Extinction of Life," "Pain: Physical or mental suffering," and "Autopsy: Examination of a corpse."[11]

In addition, Jolie was treated as an outcast by the other students. She was teased by classmates for her glasses, braces, and still undeveloped body. She had not yet grown into her large eyes and full lips, which she believed made her look like one of Jim Henson's Muppets. Her dyed purple hair and choice of wardrobe did not help much, either. Influenced by the costumes of pop singer Michael Jackson, Jolie bought some studded black-and-red leather clothing, which she frequently wore to school. Jolie's self-esteem plummeted even further when her early attempts at modeling failed. Depressed and rejected, Jolie began to contemplate suicide.

Dealing with Depression

Jolie did not attempt suicide, but she did take on some self-destructive behaviors. At fourteen, she adopted a wild lifestyle that included slam dancing, illegal drugs, and a punk boyfriend who lived with her in her bedroom for two years. According to Jolie, her mother allowed the boy to live in her room because Bertrand believed that it would keep her uncontrollable daughter from taking risks and meeting him in dangerous places.

During this troubled time in Jolie's life, she felt that she could not connect with anyone, not even her boyfriend, with whom she

The Lee Strasberg Theatre Institute

Whenever Angelina Jolie had a problem when she was little, her mother would ask, "What are you feeling? What are you thinking? What are you doing?" Those were the questions her mother had learned to ask when she had attended the Lee Strasberg Theatre Institute. Like her mother, Jolie also went to the renowned acting school, which is considered to be the most prestigious in the United States. Many of Hollywood's biggest stars were trained at Strasberg, including Marilyn Monroe, Paul Newman, Meryl Streep, and Jack Nicholson.

Strasberg students are taught the Method acting technique. Using this technique, actors do not just pretend to feel the emotions of their characters. Instead, actors draw upon their own memories and experiences to actually feel the emotions needed for a scene.

Jolie attended the school for two years. When she quit, she said that she was too young for the Method because she did not yet have enough memories to draw on. However, Jolie continued to use what she learned, and her ability to embody her characters has won her critical acclaim.

Lee Strasberg taught Method acting to many famous actors.

Quoted in Lawrence Grobel, "The Joy of Being Jolie," *Movieline*, June 2001, p. 92.

was sexually active. She began using knives to cut herself as a way of coping with her depression. She describes this period as being a time when she could not feel anything:

> When you can't feel anything from life you walk around and you don't feel the weather, you don't feel other people; even if I had somebody near me physically it just didn't feel like anything, it didn't feel like enough, nothing ever really got inside me. So I went through a phase, yeah, where I'd cut myself because then that absolutely felt like something.[12]

Feeling the pain and seeing her own blood made her feel that she was alive. She knew that what she was doing was dangerous, however, so she hid her self-inflicted injuries from her mother. She still has scars from these cuts, including one light one along her jawline.

When Jolie talks today about this phase in her life, she acknowledges that the cutting was a part of who she was at the time. But she does not condone self-mutilation. She has publicly expressed worry that teenage girls will think that hurting themselves is cool because she did it. In 1999, Jolie appeared on the TV show *Access Hollywood* to discourage teenagers from following in her footsteps and to emphasize that far from being cool, self-mutilation is a cry for help.

A New Beginning

By the time she was sixteen, Jolie felt that she had gotten the depression and destructive behavior out of her system. She decided to make some major changes. After her sophomore year, she enrolled in an alternative program within the Beverly Hills school district. The program was for students who were struggling, and it allowed her the option of working at an accelerated pace. Jolie applied herself to her studies and graduated in 1991, a year and a half early. She broke up with her boyfriend and swore off dating, at least for awhile. Jolie wanted freedom and independence, so although she was still a minor, she moved to a studio apartment a few blocks away from her mother's home.

At sixteen, Jolie had grown both physically and emotionally since her first attempts at modeling. She had made it through the awkward early teen years and had blossomed into an exceptionally beautiful woman. Her large eyes and mouth, along with her dark, flowing hair and voluptuous body, were all part of her exotic beauty. At seventeen, Jolie had no trouble finding work and signed on with the Finesse Model Company. She modeled for the company in both London and New York. She also appeared in music videos with Meat Loaf, Lenny Kravitz, the Lemonheads, and the Rolling Stones.

The modeling and music videos paid the bills, but Jolie's focus was on acting. Her first major role was as a domineering German woman in *Room Service*, a Lee Strasberg stage production. The part was originally written for a man, but Jolie made it her own. Her father was surprised by the intensity of her performance, but he was also proud. He knew then that his daughter had real talent. Their relationship improved as Jolie began to learn from her father. Haven also helped with his sister's acting career. At the time, he was attending the University of Southern California in order to become a director. He cast Angelina in five of his student films, including one that won the prestigious George Lucas Award.

Jolie enjoyed her new success. By the time she was nineteen, she had made enough money to buy her own apartment in Los Angeles. This was especially meaningful to her because she had never lived in a home that was not rented. Finally, she had a place of her own.

Chapter 2

Success . . . and Sadness

J olie was determined to achieve success in Hollywood on her own terms. For this reason, she dropped her famous surname when she began auditioning for movie roles. (Her parents had deliberately given both her and her brother middle names that could also be used as last names.) Although Jolie knew that the Voight name could give her an advantage at auditions, she also knew that such help would come at a price. Jolie explains:

> As far back as I can remember, I was always denying that he was my father. Not because I didn't love him, I really do. It was more of an independence/rebellious thing. When you're an upstart, working with other new actors you don't want to make enemies right off the bat and I think a lot of people, for good reasons, would think that I might have some unfair advantage riding in on my family name.[13]

Angelina Jolie the Cyborg

Jolie soon landed a role in the 1993 science fiction movie *Cyborg 2: Glass Shadow* alongside veteran actor Jack Palance. In the movie, Jolie plays a seductive cyborg named Casella "Cash" Reese, who has been designed to look and act like a human but also possesses superhuman strength and a fatal secret weapon. Most of the work Jolie does in the movie revolves around violence. Jolie also appears nude from the waist up in several scenes. Never shy about her sexuality, Jolie did not regret the nudity, but she was not happy

Jolie appeared in Love Is All There Is *in 1994 after overcoming a bout of suicidal depression.*

with the movie, which received such poor prescreening reviews that it went immediately to video. After she saw the movie for the first time, Jolie went to her mother's apartment and threw up.

Plunged Back into Depression

After *Cyborg 2*, Jolie did not audition for an entire year. She was depressed and often felt that she did not want to live anymore. She remembers sitting on the floor in the living room of her new apartment crying, unable to choose what color carpet she wanted because she was not sure she would be around to see it once it was installed.

She told *Rolling Stone* magazine that at one point, she seriously considered taking her own life. She was in a New York hotel room and had planned to take sleeping pills and slit her wrists with a knife. She even went as far as to write a note to the housekeeper, telling her to call the police. But then she realized that she did not have enough sleeping pills. She thought about asking her mother to send her more, but she worried that her mother would blame herself for her daughter's death. As she lay on the bed thinking, she realized, "We can make that decision any time. And I kind of lay there with myself and thought, 'You might as well live a lot, really hard . . . because you can always walk through that door.' So I started to live as if I could die any day."[14]

Jolie returned to auditions with renewed enthusiasm and was cast in teen roles in her next few movies. In 1994, she made *Love Is All There Is*, a romantic comedy loosely based on Shakespeare's *Romeo and Juliet*. Although it got fair reviews, the movie had a delayed effect on Jolie's career, as it was not released until 1996. She then had a small role as a rebellious, drug-addicted teen in the badly reviewed crime drama *Without Evidence*. Jolie does not appear until the second half of the film, and although her performance was well done, the project was a failure.

Hackers

Jolie's next movie, the 1995 cyber-thriller, *Hackers*, gave her career a much-needed boost. In the movie, Jolie plays Kate "Acid Burn"

As tough girl Kate "Acid Burn" Libby (pictured) in Hackers, Jolie held her own as the lone woman in a male dominated cast.

Libby, the only girl in a group of teenage hackers who use their in-line skating and computer skills to save themselves from being framed for another hacker's dangerous computer virus. With her short haircut and boyish clothing, Jolie fit well into the male-dominated world of young computer hackers depicted in the movie. The script was filled with computer jargon, and in order to deliver their lines convincingly, Jolie and the other cast member had to learn about computers.

Jolie read a lot of computer books and talked with real-life computer hackers. Although she did not always understand everything, she found the information fascinating. But her favorite part of the premovie training was learning to in-line skate. Jolie especially enjoyed skating with her costar, British actor Jonny Lee Miller, with whom she soon began a romance. "Racing Jonny on rollerblades was a big part of our relationship,"[15] said Jolie.

Romance on the Set

Jolie's attraction to Miller was based on more than skating together, however. As an actor, it seemed natural to Jolie to get involved with someone who shared her career. She explains:

It's a specific type of personality that goes into this job. As actors, you have a lot in common and you expose yourselves to each other emotionally. You see into each other pretty quickly. And you have down time where you get to know each other, so it's kind of an ideal situation. You get to know each other at a really deep level.[16]

Jolie and Miller shared an apartment during the filming and even went on several trips together. But she told *Rolling Stone* reporter Chris Heath that caring about someone for the first time since she was sixteen made her feel sad, and after the movie was finished, she told Miller to pretend she was gone. The two went their separate ways for about a year, during which time Jolie had another romance, this time with one of her costars in the 1996 movie *Foxfire*.

Jonny Lee Miller

Jonny Lee Miller was still finding his way to fame when he met Angelina Jolie on the set of *Hackers* in 1994. *Hackers* was Miller's first movie, although he had appeared in episodes of several television series.

Miller was born near London on November 15, 1972. He began acting at an early age, appearing in several school productions before making his television debut in the miniseries *Mansfield Park* at age eleven. Other television shows followed, and by the time he landed the lead in *Hackers*, he was considered to be a promising young talent. Miller's big break came the following year when he appeared as the heroin-addicted Sick Boy in the critically acclaimed drama *Trainspotting*. Miller went on to make other movies, including a successful remake of *Mansfield Park* in 1999, *Wes Craven Presents: Dracula 2000*, and *Aeon Flux* in 2005.

In *Foxfire*, Jolie played Margret "Legs" Sadovsky, a mysterious drifter who unites four high school girls and helps them take revenge on an abusive teacher. While filming the movie, Jolie was surprised to find herself attracted to model-turned-actor Jenny Shimizu. Jolie said that she fell in love with Shimizu the second she saw her. The two began a well-publicized relationship, and Jolie's open bisexuality contributed to her growing reputation as a sexually promiscuous bad girl. The movie, which included a scene in which the girls give each other tattoos topless, only added to the hype. The relationship lasted for just a few months, however, and when it was over, Jolie reunited with Jonny Lee Miller.

Marriage and More Movies

Jolie and Miller were married on March 28, 1996. Jolie jokes that instead of a big white wedding, she had a small black one. The

Angelina Jolie and Hackers *costar Jonny Lee Miller became a real-life couple after making the film.*

groom was dressed from head to toe in black leather. Jolie wore black leather pants and a white shirt on which she had written Miller's name in her own blood.

Jolie did not get to spend much time with her new husband. In 1996, three of her movies were released: *Love Is All There Is*, which she had made two years earlier, *Foxfire*, and *Mojave Moon*, a confusing dark comedy in which she plays a young woman who falls for a much older man. Once again, the movie included some nude scenes, which were almost always mentioned in the critics' reviews. But the critics also remarked on Jolie's now undeniable talent. They praised her performance and often noted that she was the one redeeming part of an otherwise disappointing film.

Jolie wanted roles with more depth than the teenage fare she was being offered on the big screen, however, so she decided to make a switch to the small screen. To some, this seemed to be a step backward, but she told *Interview* magazine, "As a young woman, there are parts I'll look at that may not be in the best projects, but I'm starting out in this business and trying to figure out how I can make it work."[17]

Jolie made two critically acclaimed movies for television, both of which were released in 1997. In *True Women*, which was originally shown in two parts on CBS, Jolie plays one of three young women struggling to survive on a Texas homestead in the 1860s. In *George Wallace*, a four part miniseries for TNT, Jolie played the second wife of four-term Alabama governor George Wallace. Jolie was praised for the depth she brought to the role and for her flawless southern accent. According to the director, John Frankenheimer, Jolie "brought out the bimboish side of Cornelia, the opportunist, the vulnerability, the sorrow. You saw the loss."[18]

Jolie took a break from television to film three big-screen movies in 1997. In *Playing God*, which came out later that year, Jolie portrays the girlfriend of a smuggler, who is played by Timothy Hutton. The media speculated that the two were involved in a real-life romance. However, Jolie later said that no such romance existed and that the two were just good friends. The other two movies, *Hell's Kitchen* and *Playing by Heart*, both came out in

1998. But it was in her return to the small screen, playing the lead role in the HBO docudrama *Gia*, that Jolie found another character worthy of her talent.

Getting to Gia

Over two hundred actresses auditioned for the HBO movie, which was based on the short life of Gia Carangi, a troubled 1970s super-model. Carangi rose to fame early in her life and was gracing the covers of *Vogue* and *Cosmopolitan* magazines before she was twenty. But her often volatile temper, open bisexuality, and addiction to cocaine and heroin put an end to her modeling career. In 1986, when she was just twenty-six, Carangi became one of the first women in the United States to die of AIDs.

Jolie's similarities to Carangi made her the perfect choice for the role. Not only did Jolie look like the famous model, but she also shared her wild, restless nature. The similarities hit a little too close to home, in fact, and at first, Jolie did not want the part. "I didn't want to do it," she said. "I didn't want to go to that place. And probably because I didn't want the part, because I was scared of where it would take me, the producers knew I was right for it."[19] Jolie turned the part down four times before the producers convinced her to take it.

An Emotional Role

Once she committed herself to the role, Jolie immersed herself in it. She learned everything she could about Carangi. At first, Jolie disliked Carangi intensely. In videos, Carangi's drug addiction affected her personality, making her seem vacant and insincere, which disgusted Jolie. However, as Jolie learned more, she felt that she grew to understand the troubled model and even to love her. Jolie explains: "I think she was very lonely even though she was surrounded by people. There's a lot more to her than people saw. And she had a wild beautiful spirit. Things about her that are probably really, really crazy to people were, to me, just nor-

Portraying the tragic model/actress Gia Carangi in Gia drained Jolie emotionally and ruined her marriage.

mal. I just cared about her, She'll always be like a sister to me."[20]

Jolie admits that she could very well have gone down a destructive path as Carangi did and that her career saved her. *Gia* director Michael Cristofer explains:

Angie always says the difference between her and Gia is that she has the outlet of acting as a way of making some sense of herself, and that if she hadn't had that craft to help her deal with who she was, she feels that there would have been every possibility that she could have had the spiral-out-of-control existence that Gia did have.[21]

The depiction of Gia's turbulent life included a fair amount of nudity, but Jolie did not shy away from these scenes. In fact, she has said that the physical nudity was not difficult; it was the emotional nudity—the baring of her soul—that was challenging. Jolie did not just act the part of Gia, she strove to embody her, to as much as possible become her. Once she starts filming a movie, Jolie cannot simply switch off the character at the end of the work day. For her, the character she is portraying becomes her life during the shoot. Jolie's dedication to becoming Gia took a huge toll on her emotionally.

It also took a toll on her marriage. Jolie did not see or talk to Miller while she was filming *Gia*. "When I go off to work, I become a different person, and I'm not the woman he knows," said Jolie. "When I was doing *Gia*, I disappeared for awhile and he couldn't really talk to me."[22]

Drained and Depressed

By the time Jolie had finished filming *Gia*, she and Miller had separated. Jolie still loved Miller, but she felt too depressed to be a good wife for him. According to Jolie, "I was in a place in my life where I had everything you thought you should have that would make you happy, and I was feeling emptier. I thought after *Gia* that I had given everything I had to offer. I didn't find myself growing, and I didn't have the strength to deal with it."[23] Jolie decided to

The Hit Man Story

Angelina Jolie has said in several interviews that she got so depressed while attending film school in New York that she actually tried to hire a hit man to kill her. She thought that hiring someone to make her death look like it had happened as part of a robbery would be better than committing suicide, because then no one close to her would feel guilty about not preventing her from taking her own life. Once she figured out how to withdraw from the bank the large sum of money it would cost without arousing suspicion, she contacted a hit man. Jolie tried to convince him to kill her, but according to Jolie, the man told her to think about it for a month and then call him back if she still wanted to go through with it. By the time the month had passed, Jolie was feeling better about her life and had decided to return to Hollywood. She never called the man back.

abandon her acting career. She bought an apartment in New York and enrolled at New York University as a film major. Her head had been shaved for the final scenes in *Gia*, and her hair was still very short, which made her somewhat anonymous. She did not have any friends in New York, and people rarely recognized her. She was lonely and depressed during this period and spent most of her time on the subway, in classes, or alone in her apartment.

By the end of 1997, Jolie realized that she did not want to be in New York anymore. She decided to leave film school and return to Hollywood. She missed acting, and she had also come to recognize that she could learn much more on a movie set than in a classroom. "There you were sitting on a set with someone like (director) John Frankenheimer and you could have asked him a hundred things; then suddenly you're sitting in a class with a hundred people. God I'm stupid—I was right there,"[24] said Jolie.

Angelina is all smiles after garnering the Best Supporting Actress Golden Globe Award for her role in **George Wallace.**

Praise for Angelina

Jolie's mood improved dramatically when she returned to Hollywood, and it was lifted further early in 1998 when she won a Golden Globe Award for her work in *George Wallace*. She attended the ceremony with her mother, brother, and father, who was nominated for a supporting role in *The Rainmaker*. Afterward, Jolie thrilled the media by jumping into the hotel's swimming pool in her designer gown.

Later that year, *Gia* was aired on HBO, which brought more praise for Jolie as well as a second Golden Globe Award, a Screen Actors Guild Award, and an Emmy nomination. Jolie was ecstatic about the honors, but what made her really happy was realizing that people understood Carangi and thus, in many ways, understood her as well. Jolie no longer felt alone in the world.

Jolie's career was beginning to blossom, but her marriage was coming to an end. Jolie and Miller were divorced on February 3, 1999. Jolie felt that she needed to put her energy into her career and that she could not devote herself to being the kind of wife that Miller deserved. The breakup was amicable, and the two remained close friends. "I have no regrets about our marriage—divorcing Jonny was probably the dumbest thing I've ever done," Jolie said in a 2004 interview. "He's the greatest husband a girl could ask for—we were simply too young."[25]

Chapter 3

The Next Big Thing

Jolie's success in *Gia* resulted in more media exposure than she had received before. Although the articles mentioned her talent, they tended to focus on her unconventional upbringing, fascination with knives, and famous father, not to mention her striking beauty and sexuality. The pictures that accompanied the articles often showed her in tight black leather—and not much of that. According to Jolie, every time she went to a photo shoot, the photographer would hand her something sexy to put on.

In addition, Jolie was also becoming known for her many tattoos. She began to get tattoos in her teens and says that each one has a special meaning. Jolie's first tattoo was of the Japanese symbol for death, which she got on her left shoulder so that whenever she looked over her shoulder it would remind her to live. She also had a small blue window on her spine. She got the tattoo because she said she has spent her life looking out of windows and wishing she were somewhere else (This tattoo has since been covered with one of a tiger). The small, stylized letter *h* is for her brother, James Haven. Other tattoos include two Native American symbols, two dragons, and the Latin phrase "*Quod me nutrit me destruit*," which means "What nourishes me, destroys me."

More Exposure for Jolie

Soon after *Gia* was aired, two movies that Jolie had filmed in 1997 were released. In *Hell's Kitchen*, Jolie plays Gloria, a young woman living in a violent and drug-ridden area of New York City. The film received scathing reviews that even Jolie could not

One of Jolie's many tattoos can be seen in this photo from a British awards ceremony.

escape. Jolie fared better in *Playing by Heart*, a star-studded romantic comedy in which she plays Joan, one of eleven inter-related characters who struggle to find and understand love. In their reviews, many critics singled Jolie out for praise. *Chicago Sun-Times* critic Roger Ebert said, "As the movie circled from one story to another, I found myself waiting for Angelina Jolie to come 'round again. With her pouty lips and punk chic look, she's an original."[26]

Playing by Heart may have given Jolie's career a little boost, but her work in *Gia* is widely considered to be the breakout role that led Jolie to higher-profile movies. The recognition she received meant she could be more selective about the roles she took. Although movies aimed at young people were popular during that time, Jolie did not want to be typecast into playing teenagers. She liked the complexity of older characters and wanted to play roles that reflected sides of her own personality.

Pushing Tin

Jolie found such a role in *Pushing Tin*, her first project after leaving film school. She played Mary Bell, the young and sexy wife of a competitive air traffic controller. Jolie was happy to be back in Hollywood and was pleased to be taking a lighter role than the one she had in *Gia*. "*Pushing Tin* came along just as I was coming out of my dark period," said Jolie. "I was really very happy on that set. It was free, it was fun. I had fun with the character, not to mention great people around me."[27] Those people included Billy Bob Thornton, who played her husband; John Cusack, who played a rival air traffic controller; and Cate Blanchett, who played his wife.

Jolie describes her character as "the bad girl, who drinks a lot and is really sexy and really cool and sleeps around." She said on *The View*, a morning talk show, that she was similar to Mary Bell because they are both very sexual. But she did not admire her character. In an interview with *Allure* magazine, Jolie contrasts her role to the one played by Cate Blanchett: "But in the end, the woman who's with the children at home and supports the hus-

Angelina Jolie and Billy Bob Thornton married for real after playing a husband and wife in Pushing Tin.

band is the strongest. And all of my traits [as Mary Bell] that could be considered the cool girl are really . . . I think she's really quite a pathetic character."[28]

Getting to Know Billy Bob Thornton

Jolie first met Billy Bob Thornton on the set of *Pushing Tin* in an elevator. Thornton recalls, "We came out of the elevator and I just remember . . . you know wanting something to not go away? Wishing the elevator had gone to China. It's like a bolt of lightning."[29] Jolie also felt the attraction; in fact, she reports that she was so dazed after the meeting that she ran into a wall. But she did not know that Thornton was attracted to her and did not consider a romantic relationship to be a possibility, since Thornton was engaged to actress Laura Dern.

Jolie's relationship to Thornton was limited to friendship during the filming of *Pushing Tin*. The two talked often and shared some dinners, though they were usually accompanied by others. Although they were not romantically involved, Jolie admitted to Jay Leno in a 1999 interview that she enjoyed the kissing scenes with Thornton and that she thought he was romantic and sexy. When the filming was finished, the two parted ways, and Jolie went on to film her next movie, *The Bone Collectors*.

Drawn to the Roles

Jolie accepted the role of a police officer in *The Bone Collectors* because it was a part she could relate to. She has said in several interviews that she does not go to a therapist because she considers her acting to be her therapy. So it is important to her to take parts that not only challenge her, but also help her grow both professionally and personally. She does this by choosing roles she can relate to. "I'm always me," says Jolie. "I choose roles I can identify with." This is one of the reasons she decided to play a police officer in the crime-thriller *The Bone Collectors*. She explains, "Amelia is definitely me, without my strength and certainty or sense of humor or wildness. The more variety of characters you can play, the more complete you are as a person."[30]

From director Phillip Noyce's point of view, Jolie was the only choice for the role. He told *Rolling Stone* magazine that he had seen her in *Gia* and felt she had the strength, vulnerability, and fearlessness needed to portray the rookie cop. In the movie, Jolie's character teams up with a quadriplegic homicide detective, played by Denzel Washington, to catch a brutal serial killer. The role of Amelia Donaghy was highly sought after, and several big-name actresses even offered to cut their fees if given the part. But even though Jolie was still not a big Hollywood star, Noyce had to have her for the role.

*Angelina Jolie, pictured with costar Denzel Washington, won rave reviews for her graceful perfomance in **The Bone Collector**.*

Although she was intrigued with the story, Jolie did not share Noyce's confidence. She was nervous about working with Washington, who was one of the most respected actors in Hollywood, and worried about the part itself. She explains, "From the beginning, I felt as if I was not capable of doing this, of leading a film and being responsible for this [role]."[31]

Just as in her other roles, Jolie researched the part thoroughly. She went to forensic labs and looked at graphic pictures of crime scenes and murder victims. Even though the pictures made her sick to her stomach, she kept several of them posted above her desk in her trailer during the filming because that is what a real police officer would do.

Although the movie was difficult for Jolie, the result was worth the emotional turmoil. Jolie was praised for her graceful portrayal of Amelia and for the complexity she brought to the character. Noyce recalls a test screening that took place in Paramus, New Jersey. After the film, he says, "The audience couldn't stop raving about Angelina. Finally, Washington couldn't resist shouting out, 'And what about Denzel? Don't you think he was great?'"[32]

In her next movie, *Girl, Interrupted*, Jolie played a very different kind of character. The grace and sensitivity of Amelia were replaced with the blunt, uninhibited wildness of charismatic sociopath Lisa Rowe.

Relating to Lisa

Girl, Interrupted, which was released at the end of 1999, was based on the memoirs of Susannah Kaysan, who wrote about her time in a mental institution in the late 1960s, when she was eighteen years old. Kaysan's story was brought to the big screen by actress Winona Ryder, who stars in the movie. Ryder had seen *Gia* and felt that Jolie would be right for the role of Lisa.

Jolie also felt she was perfect for the part. After she had read the script, she found her own copy of the book, which she had read five years earlier as a teenager. She opened the book to find that she had underlined everything that had to do with Lisa. During an interview with *Premiere* magazine, Jolie explained how

Girl, Interrupted resulted in an Oscar for Jolie, who appears here in a scene from the movie with Winona Ryder (right).

she identified with Lisa by showing the interviewer one of her tattoos, a Tennessee Williams quote that says, "A prayer for the wild at heart kept in cages." Several other actresses had auditioned for the part, but according to director James Marigold, "No one who auditioned could bring Lisa to life until Jolie. Angie walked in one day, sat down and was Lisa."[33]

On and Off the Set

Girl, Interrupted was filmed in an old, mostly unused mental hospital in Harrisburg, Pennsylvania. In the movie, Jolie's character is the magnetic though often cruel ringleader of a small group of mentally ill girls. As usual, Jolie did not leave her character on the set. Like Lisa, Jolie seemed to attract other people to her. After work, her trailer was the scene of a nonstop party. "I don't really have girlfriends," said Jolie. "But it was nice. We'd all hang out in the trailer and talk and take road trips."[34]

Although she socialized with other people, she did not get too close to them. Jolie stayed in character, which meant she could not allow herself to care about the people around her. This is why the camaraderie did not extend to Ryder, who also stayed in character throughout the shoot. In her article in *Premiere* magazine, Trish Deitch Rohrer explains their relationship: "There was something about the characters that made it almost impossible for Ryder and Jolie to connect socially: Jolie had come to *Girl, Interrupted* expecting, as Lisa, to become very depressed; but she discovered to her surprise, that what Lisa felt was nothing. Not a thing. Ryder, on the other hand, felt everything."[35]

Lisa On-Screen

Jolie was fascinated with her role as Lisa. She was drawn to the uninhibited and impulsive way that Lisa lived her life and felt she understood the character's motivation. "Lisa is somebody who lives completely on impulse," Jolie says. "She's very angry at people for not being who they are—for living with masks on, in love with their own problems. She just wants to shake everybody."[36]

Although she understood Lisa, Jolie worried that other people would not. She was unhappy with the final cut of the film, which she felt showed no compassion for her character. She explains, "At the end of the film there's a certain sense of them saying to Lisa, 'Nobody wants you to live, nobody likes the way you are—you'd be better off if you were sedated and tied down and shut up.'"[37] Jolie identified so strongly with her character that she took these messages personally and felt as though they were directed at her. Once again, Jolie fell into depression and questioned her self-worth. She felt better when the film was released and people did express compassion for Lisa, despite the way the movie portrayed her.

James Haven: Angelina Jolie's Supportive Big Brother

Angelina Jolie's older brother, James Haven, has been present to encourage Jolie in her low times and celebrate with her when things were going well. When Jolie won her Golden Globe award for *George Wallace,* she insisted that he accompany her onstage while she made her acceptance speech. Haven's support for his younger sister has never wavered, despite the fact that he has not been nearly as successful as she in his own acting career.

Haven remembers visiting his father, Jon Voight, on movie sets when he was little and knowing that he wanted to be an actor, too. Unlike Jolie, Haven completed film school, graduating from the University of Southern California in 1995. Since then, he has had small parts in several of Jolie's films, and even one of Thornton's in 2001. Other work includes a series of appearances on the television show *CSI,* a starring role in a critically acclaimed short, and a lead role in a poorly reviewed 2004 film called *Breaking Dawn.*

Jolie's brother James Haven is her number one supporter.

Roses for Jolie

Just hours after accepting her Oscar for *Girl, Interrupted*, Angelina Jolie had to fly back to Mexico, where she was shooting the movie *Original Sin*. She got back at about four in the morning and was asleep in her trailer when she was awakened by a mariachi band playing outside. She stumbled out of her trailer to find the entire cast and crew of the movie assembled outside, each holding a single rose. One at a time, each person gave Jolie a rose, until she had about two hundred of them.

The tribute was especially meaningful to Jolie because many of the people in the crew, including the director, Michael Cristofer, had also worked on *Gia* three years ealier. They had seen the toll that playing Gia had taken on her and were thrilled that her talent had finally been acknowledged with an Oscar.

The actress proudly displays her Oscar.

The Next Big Thing

Girl, Interrupted was produced by Columbia Pictures, which had high expectations for the film. In order to position the movie for the Academy Awards, the studio delayed releasing it until late December 1999. By this time, *Pushing Tin* and *The Bone Collectors* had both been released, and Jolie had become a Hollywood favorite. She was featured in dozens of articles, graced the covers of several magazines, and was constantly being called the "It girl" and the "next big thing." While others were impressed, Jolie herself was not. When asked what it was like to be the next big thing, she replied, "I'm a thing? I think we all know that everybody is the Next Big Thing . . . and then they're not."[38]

Despite the hype surrounding it, *Girl, Interrupted* opened to mixed reviews. Although Jolie's part was a supporting role to Ryder's lead, Lisa was such a domineering presence that she often overshadowed Ryder's more reserved character. Much to the disappointment of Columbia executives, *Girl, Interrupted* received only one Oscar nomination, and it was for Jolie as Best Supporting Actress. She also won Golden Globe and Screen Actors Guild awards for her work in the film.

An Oscar for Angelina

Jolie went to the Academy Awards ceremony with her brother, James Haven. The two spent so much time on the red carpet answering questions that they were locked out of the auditorium for the first twenty minutes of the show. Jolie was frantic because in years past, the first award presented had been the one for Best Supporting Actress. Jolie assumed that she was going to miss the announcement. She begged the usher to let her and Haven in. As it turned out, however, the order of the awards had been changed, and Best Supporting Actress was not presented first.

When Jolie's name was announced as the winner, she was so excited that she embraced her brother and kissed him on the mouth before going to accept the award. In her speech, she excitedly thanked her parents and people she had worked with on the movie. She also heaped praises on her brother, saying, "I'm so in love with my brother right now . . . I have nothing without you. You're the most amazing man I've ever known and I love you."[39]

The kiss, along with her affectionate sentiments toward her brother in her acceptance speech, started a huge wave of speculation about her relationship with him. People said that the two were involved romantically. Both Jolie and Haven were shocked and saddened by the accusations, which they both denied. Jolie told *Movieline* magazine:

> It was extremely sad because it was just an example of a love between siblings. A simple, normal love. . . . If it seemed like a real kiss, it was probably because we held each other too long, but there was nothing but a pure love. When I said, "I'm so in love with my brother," it was me very honestly saying, "Right in this moment, I'm in love with this guy sitting right here because he's so wonderful and supportive of his sister" and he loved me in that moment. Which is very rare . . . and very special.[40]

In another interview with *Talk* magazine, Jolie used her own wild reputation as her defense, saying, "The funny thing about this rumor with my brother is that if I was, in fact, doing that, I'd say it. Everyone knows that about me!"[41]

What she did not tell the media at the time was that the real love of her life was Billy Bob Thornton. The two were secretly seeing each other, and Jolie even managed a quick visit with him after the awards. With an Oscar in hand and a budding romance, Jolie was proving that she really was the next big thing.

Chapter 4

Love and Lara

J olie was shooting *Original Sin* with Antonio Banderas in Mexico when she received her Oscar. While filming the movie, Jolie made frequent trips to Los Angeles to see Billy Bob Thornton. It is unclear exactly when their friendship turned romantic, but according to Banderas, Jolie did not hide the fact that she was falling in love with Thornton. At one point, she even said, "I want to marry this man. I don't think there's anybody who could love him more."[42]

Shortly before they were wed, Jolie had a kind of breakdown. She told *Rolling Stone* that she thought she had lost Thornton. After meeting her mother at the airport in Los Angeles, Jolie broke down in tears and could not stop crying. Soon she could not speak either. Her mother called a doctor and she was admitted to a mental hospital. Later she said that this was a meaningful experience because *Girl, Interrupted* had recently been released, and several of the patients there had seen it. Jolie felt that it was reassuring to the other patients to realize that even people who seem to have a perfect life have problems. Jolie's mother located Thornton and told him what had happened. He rushed to Jolie's side, and a few days later, they were married.

Wed to Billy Bob Thornton

Jolie and Thornton were married on May 5, 2000, in blue jeans at the Little Church of the West in Las Vegas, Nevada. The media had a field day with the unexpected wedding. Although people close to the couple had known about the romance, it was a surprise to most, including Thornton's fiancée, Laura Dern, who told

Never shy about their relationship, Jolie and Thornton share a kiss for the cameras.

Talk magazine that she found out she was no longer engaged to Thornton by reading about his wedding in the tabloids.

For the most part, the media did not have good things to say about the union. Thornton was already the father of two children, and he was twenty years older than Jolie. He was not new to marriage either; Jolie was his fifth wife. In addition, Thornton had an eccentric reputation that even managed to outstrip his new wife's. The country boy-turned-movie star had fears of flying, Komodo dragons, and antique furniture; had admitted to struggles with alcohol and eating disorders; and had obsessive-compulsive tendencies. In addition, like his wife, he boasted several tattoos.

The media had plenty to write about because Jolie and Thornton were not shy about sharing their feelings for each other. The couple was openly affectionate and often publicly engaged in long, passionate kisses. They also never missed an opportunity to tell the press about their intense passion and admiration for one another. "I'm madly in love with this man and I will be till the day I die,"[43] said Jolie.

Blood Rituals

But perhaps the most bizarre part of their relationship was their use of their own blood to demonstrate their devotion to one another. "Like a lot of couples, you always talk about how much in love with each other you are and you can't think of enough ways to devour each other and take each other. And blood is your life,"[44] said Jolie. The most well-known blood tribute was the glass vials that they wore as necklaces. For their first Christmas together, Jolie bought two glass amulets that were originally meant to hold pressed flowers. Jolie cut her finger and dripped a little blood into one of the amulets, and Thornton did the same. They traded amulets and were rarely seen without them. Thornton also used his blood to sign a notarized pledge stating that he would never leave Jolie. For her part, Jolie wrote "To the End of Time" above their bed in her blood. The two also got tattoos of each other's names, and for their first anniversary, Jolie bought them adjoining cemetery plots.

Although their relationship was intense and wild, it also had a calming effect on Jolie, who had felt empty and unsettled before she met Thornton. In an online interview shortly after her wedding, she said, "Now I'm completely calm and I feel I have so much meaning in my life and I'm so clear and he's just made me complete. I just admire him and have so much fun with him."[45]

The two lived together in a Beverly Hills mansion that had previously belonged to heavy metal guitarist Slash from the group Guns n' Roses. Jolie loved spending time at home with Thornton, but she also loved making movies. With her new Oscar, Jolie had her pick of projects.

Fun with Cars

Although many people told her she should stick to serious films since she had just won the Oscar, Jolie wanted to do something lighter. She turned down the chance to be one of Charlie's Angels in order to take a much smaller part in the action-thriller *Gone in Sixty Seconds*. The director had told Jolie that being an "angel" would be fun and that it would make her a big star, but superstardom did not hold much appeal for Jolie, and the movie did not sound like her kind of fun. She did not want to get dressed up and wear high heels, and she did not think she would fit in well with the other two female leads, Cameron Diaz and Drew Barrymore.

In *Gone in Sixty Seconds*, Jolie played Sara "Sway" Wayland, part of a gang of car thieves who must steal fifty exotic cars in a single night. For the part, Jolie was trained in stunt driving by legendary stunt driver Bobby Orr, and she also learned how to hot-wire a car. Jolie enjoyed driving the cars and feeling like she was part of a team during the filming. As expected, the movie got mediocre reviews but was popular at the box office.

Jolie was still not ready to take on a serious role again like that of Gia or Lisa, but she did want a role that would be interesting and challenging. She found that challenge by accepting the lead role in the big-budget adventure movie *Lara Croft: Tomb Raider*.

Thornton Sings About Jolie

Billy Bob Thornton was forty-three years old and already well into a successful Hollywood career when he met Angelina Jolie in 1998. By the time he married Jolie two years later, he was branching out into writing and singing country music. In 2001, he released his first CD, *Private Radio.* The CD included a song called "*Angelina,*" in which he addressed the popular public opinion that their marriage would not last with the lyrics: "They all said we'd never make it / Two crazy panthers on the prowl / They said we would only fake it for awhile / But we just looked at them and growled." Thornton went on to make two more CDs, but he did not find the same success with his music that he had with his acting and writing.

Thornton and his band sing about Jolie at the House of Blues.

Billy Bob Thornton, "Angelina," *Private Radio*, Lonesome Highway Records, September 25, 2001.

Quest for Adventure

Lara Croft was originally created as the heroine in the popular video game *Tomb Raider*. When Jolie was first approached about playing the character in a movie inspired by the game, she did not want to do it because she thought it would be campy and silly. But when director Simon West told her that the writers were going to flesh out her character and give her real emotions and relationships, she started to find the role intriguing. She liked the idea that Lara was athletic and strong but also very feminine, with long hair and plenty of curves. The character was smart and in control of her life, which also appealed to Jolie.

Becoming Lara Croft

Jolie's tendency to blur the lines between herself and the characters she plays was essential for her role in *Tomb Raider.* "I think we realized early on that because of what type of character Lara is, you can't pretend to be her, you have to be her," said Jolie. "Like you can't pretend to do the stunts, and wear the guns and shoot them, and just run around like that. The character has to actually do those things."[46] Actually doing those things required a great deal of training before the filming even began.

Jolie arrived at the Pinewood Studios in England two and a half months before the first scene was shot. The wine and cigarettes she had gotten used to while shooting *Gone in Sixty Seconds* were banished, as was all sugar and caffeine. A nutritionist fed Jolie five high-protein meals a day to help her build muscle and maintain a high level of energy for her rigorous training schedule. Not only did Jolie have to get her body into top physical shape, but she also had to learn some new skills. Jolie had lessons in street fighting, kickboxing, weapons, bungee ballet, dogsledding, stunt diving, and yoga. In addition, she was trained in English etiquette and learned to speak with an upper-class British accent.

Jolie surprised West by not only wanting to do her own stunts, but also doing many of them better than the trained stunt doubles. West had originally planned on using Jolie only for some of the easier stunt sequences, but when he discovered what she

A movie poster for Lara Croft: Tomb Raider shows the sexy video game character Jolie brought to life.

could do, he let her do almost all of them, despite the fact that many of them were dangerous. "Angelina was doing triple back flips on the set. She was doing the bungee jumps from fifty feet up in the air. She was laughing. The stunt doubles were clinging to their safety ropes," said West. "For one scene where Lara surfs through the air on a thin log, her stunt double refused to do it. Angie said 'no problem.' Within a week, she was going 'I love it! Let's go again!'"[47]

Although she enjoyed the physical challenges of the role, there were many times when it was not so pleasant. Jolie suffered from several physical injuries as well as the occasional lack of confidence. She got numerous cuts and bruises from the harnesses and bungee cords; she dislocated a shoulder, tore a ligament in

As Lara Croft, Jolie rides a swinging pillar like a surfboard. The actress did most of her own stunts.

her ankle, and burned herself while hanging from a chandelier. At times she doubted she could do the part. "One night I was sitting in my bathtub with my bruises and cuts," said Jolie. "I was crying and thinking 'What am I doing? I can't pull this off. I can't even keep the guns straight. I keep hitting myself with her stupid braid.'"[48] But as she got into better shape, she found herself making fewer mistakes and began to feel proud of her accomplishments.

Reconnecting with Dad

Another person who was proud of her accomplishments was Jolie's father, who had the role of Lara's father in the movie. "Obviously I'm very proud of Angie," said Voight. "I've been very impressed with her professional understandings and her insights into character. I've been actually a little dazzled by it."[49] Jolie thought her father would be perfect for the role, and she asked him to take it because she felt that Lara's relationship with her father was similar to her own. Like Lara, Jolie also followed her father into his career. Also like Lara, she felt her father's influence in her life, even though he was not around much during her childhood.

Jolie and Voight had only one scene together, but it was an emotional one for Jolie. Even though they were acting, the two used the scene to communicate to each other. According to Jolie, "It was very, very personal to me because it is my dad and we adjusted little things, maybe a word here or there, so we were really speaking to each other."[50]

Tomb Raider was Jolie and Voight's first movie together since she was a child. Jolie was delighted to find that she really enjoyed acting with her father. "It was . . . fun to suddenly look up to your dad and you're both in costumes with accents—playing and being actors and doing what you both love. It was very moving,"[51] said Jolie. The two connected off the set as well. Jolie talked to Voight about her role and the challenges it presented, and Voight offered his daughter encouragement and advice. At the time, Jolie was thrilled to have her father's support and felt that they had finally come together as father and daughter.

Far from Home

Another aspect of the movie that Jolie enjoyed was shooting on location in Cambodia. Although he could have shot the entire movie in England, West wanted to shoot in exotic locations that were not often seen in movies. He chose Angkor Wat, Cambodia, for its ancient ruins and traditional culture. Jolie was surprised by how deeply the trip affected her. She fell in love with the country and its people, and she was moved by what she learned about the challenges people in that part of the world face. She had not known that unexploded land mines were a huge problem in Cambodia. The mines, which were left over from thirty years of warfare, were often planted in fields, along roads, or near schools. She saw many people who had lost limbs to land mines. She saw people living in poverty much worse than anything she had seen in the United States. Jolie said the trip opened her eyes to how people in underdeveloped countries live.

Parts of the movie were also shot in Iceland, but Jolie did not like that as much, mostly because she does not like cold weather. She did, however, enjoy getting to feel like an explorer as the crew crossed desolate and often dangerous ice fields, and she loved the dogsledding scenes.

Throughout the shoot, Jolie found it extremely difficult to be away from Thornton, whose fear of flying kept him from making the trans-Atlantic trip. Jolie flew back to Los Angeles when she could, but usually she had to settle for phone calls, during which she often broke down in tears. At least once, Thornton called when she was on the set. All action stopped as Jolie engaged in an emotional conversation with her husband.

Trouble for *Tomb Raider*

Jolie was aware that *Tomb Raider* carried some very high expectations, both from the studio and the fans. The budget for the film was $80 million, more than that of any other film Jolie had worked on, so it would have to be successful for the studio to recoup this amount and make a profit. Studio executives also hoped that *Tomb Raider* would become the first in a profitable

At Home with Angelina Jolie and Billy Bob Thornton

When Angelina Jolie and Billy Bob Thornton set up housekeeping together, they did things in their own way. Jolie preferred to bake cakes and cookies in a toy Easy Bake oven rather than a real one. Their living room featured a hanging bubble chair, a shrine to Elvis Presley, and a life-size plastic horse that could be sat on to watch television. The spare bedroom was kept locked because it housed part of Jolie's knife collection—about thirty knives, some from her movies and some from remote places around the world. The couple also had a mynah bird and a pet rat named Harry that lived in a cage in their bedroom. They wanted to get a pet beaver, but could not because it is illegal to keep a wild animal. They also had plans to install a fire pole that would go from the bedroom down to the kitchen, empty the pool in the backyard and fill it with plastic balls, and get a poodle. These plans were never completed, however.

series. In addition, the video game had a loyal following of fans. Because Jolie was the lead in the movie, much of its success or failure rested on her shoulders. "It's a big responsibility," said Jolie. "Those fans are expecting that they are going to see a character they know so well, this character they love. So you have a lot to live up to, and there's always the anxiety of not being able to pull that off."[52]

In many ways, Jolie did successfully embody the role of Lara Croft, but despite her best efforts, the movie did not do nearly as well as anticipated. Although most critics were impressed with the exotic locations and elaborate sets, they did not think much of the movie itself. Critics complained that the story line, which was fine for a video game, was silly and confusing on the big screen. Many felt that the characters were poorly developed and that the action sequences were meaningless and at times even boring, like watching someone else play a video game. When the critics commented on Jolie, their remarks usually had more to do with her body than with her acting ability. Critics frequently mentioned her ample chest and skintight clothing. The film was not a complete failure, however; despite the poor reviews, it made $130 million, enough of a profit to assure Jolie a sequel.

Just a month later, in late July, *Original Sin* came out to even more disappointing reviews. Jolie, however, had other things to think about. Her time in Cambodia had made her realize that there are more important things in life than movie reviews.

Chapter 5

Changing Priorities

Jolie did not forget her experiences in Cambodia when she returned to the United States after shooting *Tomb Raider*. She was struck by the contrast between the affluent American lifestyle and the poverty and suffering she saw in Cambodia. In an interview with *GQ* magazine, Jolie explains:

> I thought I knew what suffering was. I had no idea what suffering was. I had never seen real poverty. And I had never met people like that. People who had been through war, genocide, occupation. People whose children had their legs blown off thirty years after the war had ended by land mines that had been waiting for them in the soil—but who still had humor and grace. I couldn't understand why I hadn't read about these . . . things in my history books in school. I was angry and ashamed at what I didn't know. It's not that I suddenly wanted to "help." More that I had a sudden need to find out what else I didn't know.[53]

Jolie took on the task of learning everything she could about Cambodia. She read books, atlases, and United Nations (UN) reports. She found herself most drawn to the information about refugees—people who had been forced to leave their homes because of war, earthquakes, or other catastrophic events. She felt these people, who number over 20 million worldwide and who have no homes, almost no possessions, and often no families, were more vulnerable than any other group. She wanted to learn more.

Jolie decided to contact the UN. She was directed to the Office of the United Nations High Commissioner on Refugees (UNHCR) in Washington, D.C. When Jolie told UNHCR officials that she wanted to learn about refugees in Cambodia as well as in other parts of the world, they invited her to Washington. Jolie went, without Thornton, who was busy with his music.

Traveling with the UNHCR

In Washington, Jolie met with UNHCR officials, who gave her more details about the refugee situation in Cambodia as well as other countries. Jolie wanted to learn more, she wanted to help. In February 2001, she was invited to travel with the UNHCR to Ivory Coast, Tanzania, and Sierra Leone. Thornton did not want his wife to go, because he thought it would be dangerous. But he also did not offer to accompany her. Jolie's father also did not want her to go and even called the UNHCR to try to get her trip canceled. But Jolie was determined.

Throughout the trip, Jolie kept a journal. In it, she wrote about the people she met and the challenges that the UNHCR faces, such as underfunding, poor conditions in refugee camps, and violence from rebel groups. She also wrote about her own feelings and impressions. On the first page, she wrote, "I honestly want to help. I don't believe I am different from other people. I think we all want justice and equality. We all want a chance for a life with meaning. All of us would like to believe that if we were in a bad situation someone would help us."[54]

During the trip, Jolie met with UNHCR workers to discuss the refugee situations in the countries she visited. She went to UNHCR camps, where she met refugees and heard their stories. Most of these people came from places where war had destroyed their homes and everything they owned. Many had been victims of horrible war crimes and had suffered trauma and serious injuries. All had lost family members. The camps were overcrowded and underfunded, and they did not have nearly enough food, clothing, and medical supplies. Jolie worked right alongside the UNHCR workers. She distributed food, measured medicines, comforted sick children, and offered assistance to refugees in whatever ways she could.

Jolie, who insisted on paying for all the expenses associated with her trip, did not receive or even want special treatment because she was famous. She shared the same living quarters as the UNHCR workers. She stayed in utilitarian UN apartments and hot, often dirty, hotel rooms, sometimes without electricity. She ate the same sparse, simple meals as the UNHCR workers and traveled in unreliable trucks on bumpy and often dangerous roads. Jolie did not complain; instead, she was grateful for the accommodations, which she knew were much better than the living conditions of the refugees who lived in the camps. In her journal, Jolie wrote about a UNHCR guesthouse:

Jolie greets Cambodia's prime minister. The nation granted the actress citizenship in recognition of her work there.

Broken glass is stuck into the top of the cement walls that surround the house.

As our truck pulls up, a guard opens the wooden gate.

A small, off-white building with chipped paint and a few old cars stands beyond the gate.

I am greeted with smiles by most, stares by a few.

I am in room number 1. That's what the piece of paper stuck to my door says. I think they gave me the best they have.

I could hardly get water out of the shower. The room would be considered poor and run-down by the people from the world I live in, but certainly not by the people here. They would consider it a palace.

I am very grateful.[55]

The trip had a significant effect on Jolie. She found herself flooded with mixed emotions. She felt ashamed of her comfortable American lifestyle and of her ignorance about what had been happening in other parts of the world. The stories the refugees told, and the conditions they lived in, made her feel sad and angry. She found that she felt a deep sense of admiration and respect for the refugees and the people who dedicate their lives to helping them. She admired the refugees' courage and their ability to live with grace and kindness, even when their lives had been destroyed. Jolie also felt a change in herself. On the plane home, she wrote, "These three weeks have been a new world for me— a special time—I have changed. I like who I became here."[56]

Ambassador Jolie

Jolie took two more trips with the UNHCR in 2001. In July, she returned to Cambodia, and in August, she visited Pakistan. In

Notes from My Travels

In 2003, Angelina Jolie published her journals from four of her trips with the UNHCR in a book titled *Notes from My Travels*. Jolie's proceeds from the book, which was released with little publicity, were donated to the UNHCR. Her journal entries include stories about what she saw and did and challenges that the UNHCR faces, as well as her own feelings about what she learned. The book received mostly positive reviews and was endorsed by renowned primatologist and UN messenger of peace Jane Goodall, who said, "I was deeply moved by her descriptions of individual refugees struggling to live with dignity and hope, and found her personal commitment to be an inspiration."

Quoted in Angelina Jolie, *Notes from My Travels*. New York: Simon and Schuster, 2003, back cover.

Cambodia, the conditions were even worse than on her previous trip. She met hundreds of people who had been seriously injured by land mines and yet continued to try and earn a living and care for their families. Jolie was amazed by their kindness and bravery. In Pakistan, Jolie met refugees from Afghanistan, who told her about the oppressive violence of the Taliban, a fundamentalist Islamic sect that ruled Afghanistan from 1996 to 2001.

When Jolie was in Cambodia, she was asked to be a goodwill ambassador for the UNHCR. The UNHCR officials were impressed with her dedication in the field and hoped she could use her celebrity status to bring attention to the refugee situation and inspire other people to help. Jolie was honored to be chosen for the position but also a little worried that her brand of fame might be more damaging to the UNHCR than helpful. According to Jolie, "I actually sat them down and said, 'You do realize that people think I'm strange?' There are a lot of rumors about me, and I said, 'Do you really want me? Getting me involved might damage your reputation.'"[57]

The United Nations High Commissioner, Rudd Lubbers, was not worried about Jolie's reputation. "We are very pleased that Ms. Jolie has generously agreed to give her time and energy to support UNHCR's work," he said. "She can help give a voice to refugees, many of whom live in the shadows of forgotten tragedies. We are proud to welcome her to the UNHCR family."[58] On August 27, 2001, at a ceremony in Geneva, Switzerland, Jolie became a goodwill ambassador for the UNHCR.

Making a Difference Around the World

Jolie has taken her appointment seriously. She has traveled to more than twenty countries, often to dangerous and desolate areas, to help with UNHCR projects. She has met with senior government officials in several countries to lobby for refugee rights. She takes a major role in World Refugee Day each year, hosting events, giving speeches, and sponsoring a national poster contest for schoolchildren in the United States. In addition, she has started several charitable foundations to raise funds for UNHCR's causes. She has already given over $8 million of her own money and has pledged to donate a third of her future income. She is often one of the first private donors to come forward when emergency funds are needed. She aided refugees after the 2004 tsunami and the 2005 Pakistan earthquake. Jolie has received several awards for her humanitarian work, including the United Nations Correspondents Association's Citizen of the World Award in 2003 and the Humanitarian Action Award in 2005 from the United Nations Association of the USA and the Business Council for the United Nations.

Jolie has found a sense of purpose in her humanitarian work that was lacking in her career as an actress. She explains:

> When I'm in a refugee camp, my spirit feels better there than anywhere else in the world, because I am surrounded by such truth and family. I feel so connected to just simply being a human being. In these countries, they don't know who I am. I am useful as a woman who's willing to spend a day in the dirt. Maybe it was important for me to know that.[59]

Stranded in Tanzania

Jolie told *Vogue* magazine a story about how she learned quickly that Hollywood and her humanitarian work do not always mix when she was stranded in Tanzania at the end of her first trip with the UNHCR:

I was in Tanzania on the border, and it's just this really faraway place that you take little planes to get into and then drive to the border. I didn't have any means of getting out, because somehow I was going to rough it, and then after two weeks Hollywood was going to come and get me. In a private plane, with a premiere dress, makeup, and some snacks! So I had basically given away all my money and run out of everything, including . . . clean clothes, and food. So this random message somehow came over the wire: "The premiere's canceled. Stay as long as you want. Have a good time." It was kind of like, Oh my God. I've just been left here. Hollywood doesn't need you for a premiere, so we don't care what happens to you.

Quoted in Jonathan Van Meter, "Learning to Fly," *Vogue*, March 2004, p. 175.

Motherhood

Jolie's newfound sense of purpose made her feel stable enough to do something she never thought she could: become a parent. "I always felt I wasn't going to be a mother," said Jolie. "I knew that to be a parent, nothing about me could be self destructive or unsure day to day. I never thought I could be that balanced."[60]

Jolie was not the only one who thought she was ready to become a parent. In order to adopt, she had to go through a screening process to make sure she would be a good mother. She was relieved when her own belief that she was ready for motherhood was affirmed by the screener. "With my reputation for every crazy thing in the world, it was very reassuring to have a woman analyze me and say I'm a fit parent,"[61] Jolie says.

In November 2001, Jolie returned to Cambodia with Thornton, who overcame his fear of flying to make the trip. They were there to adopt a baby from an orphanage. Jolie told *Marie Claire* magazine about how she found her son:

> I met a lot of lovely little kids but there was this one little baby who was asleep. He was put in my arms and he opened his eyes and stared at me for the longest time. Then he smiled, and I smiled back, and we both seemed cool with each other. It made me feel like I could be this baby's mom, that I could make him feel happy and safe. It was suddenly clear to me that I'd just found my best friend.[62]

Jolie could not take the baby home right away. There were medical tests and a lot of paperwork that had to be done first. She did not see the child again for four months, but in March 2002, he was brought to Namibia, where Jolie was filming her next movie, *Beyond Borders*. Jolie named him Maddox Chivan.

United Nations ambassador of goodwill Jolie distributes balls to refugee children in Thailand.

At Home in Cambodia

Shortly after adopting Maddox, Jolie began building a modest home in the jungles of northwest Cambodia. The small hut was built on stilts and is located in a remote area that is accessible only by helicopter or boat. Jolie planned to live there for part of each year because she loves the country and she wants Maddox to grow up with a sense of his own heritage. The land, which is legally owned by Maddox, had to be de-mined before the hut could be built. Forty-eight land mines were found on the property. Many of Jolie's neighbors are land mine victims.

Jolie is also helping to protect and rehabilitate wildlife in Cambodia. She has given $5 million to fund a forest conservation project that will educate villagers, train local rangers, and help protect wildlife and natural resources in the area. She has been warmly welcomed in Cambodia by both government officials and private citizens. In 2005, Jolie was given Cambodian citizenship in hopes that she will make frequent trips to the country.

Although she was still very busy and could certainly afford a nanny, Jolie chose not to hire one. Instead, she took care of Maddox, whom she calls Mad for short, almost completely by herself. She kept him close to her most of the time and refused to be apart from him for more than a few hours. Whenever she traveled for a movie or for the UNHCR, she took Maddox along with her. Like her humanitarian work, being a mother gave Jolie a sense of purpose: "It's an amazing thing to take care of a child and to have a child trust you and love you. That makes me feel like I somehow have a purpose. I didn't know what I would be like as a parent. So, I've learned that I love being a mom. If he's OK, if he's healthy, nothing else matters to me. And, that's just such a clarity. I never knew."[63]

Good-bye to Thornton

Thornton did not share Jolie's enthusiasm for parenthood. Although the couple did not admit it to the press, their marriage was in crisis. Jolie explains:

> I began to realize that he wasn't willing to take the responsibility of helping me raise Maddox. And I was very disappointed and disillusioned by that. He turned out to be far less of a man than I expected him to be. He decided to go touring with his band and focus on his music instead of staying with me and being with Maddox. I think that speaks for itself.[64]

Jolie felt that Thornton was no longer respectful of her or committed to their marriage. In June 2002, she moved out of their home and filed for divorce. The divorce was finalized on May 27, 2003. In the settlement, Jolie was given full custody of Maddox.

Despite the intensity of her relationship with Thornton, Jolie did not break down after her marriage fell apart. Instead, she focused her energy on Maddox and took solace in her friends and family. The breakup was bitter, and for a time, Jolie and Thornton did not speak to each other. But in 2004, the two rekindled their friendship, and Jolie has acknowledged that Thornton will always be an important part of her life.

Good-bye to Dad

Around the same time that Jolie was feeling disillusioned with Thornton, she was also having similar feelings about her father. Jolie's relationship with Voight started to deteriorate soon after *Tomb Raider*. According to Jolie, the connection the two shared while filming the movie was only temporary. "We seemed to understand each other and it was fun, but afterwards he returned quickly to old habits of being judgmental,"[65] she said.

Jolie and Voight's rocky relationship took center stage in August 2002, when Voight appeared on *Access Hollywood* as well as several other entertainment news shows to tearfully claim that his daughter had serious mental problems and should seek help. Jolie

The camera catches Jolie, Maddox, and Zahara shopping for children's clothes in Berlin, Germany.

denied the accusations, saying, "I may have needed therapy and help in my life but certainly not these last few years when I've adopted my son and grown up quite a lot. So maybe he's ten years too late."[66] She said Voight's actions were unforgivable because the adoption officials might have believed his accusations and taken Maddox away from her.

The last straw came soon after, when Voight went with Jolie to the airport as she was leaving for a UNHCR mission to Cambodia. According to Jolie:

> He gave me a letter in the car and said, "this is my truth, this is unchanging." I was unaware of what he'd written and said, "That's wonderful, I love you, see you later."

> Then I opened the letter. He'd written I was a bad person. I was upset and thought of 100 replies, and then decided I don't value this person's opinion so it's okay. I no longer see us as father and daughter.[67]

Jolie has severed ties with Voight and refuses all communications with him. She has also said that despite Voight's opinions of her, she knows she is a good mother, a good friend, and a good person.

Chapter 6

A Life of Purpose

After adopting Maddox and divorcing Thornton, Jolie wanted to focus her energy on parenthood and on her humanitarian work. She considered retiring from acting, but she knew that her celebrity status and high income were part of the reason she was so successful as a goodwill ambassador, so she continued to make movies, taking Maddox with her for every shoot.

Good Acting, Bad Movies

Jolie's next four movies all did poorly at the box office, a fact that puzzled critics, many of whom admired Jolie's talent. "As Angelina Jolie gets better as an actress, her films get worse. It's not supposed to work that way,"[68] observed movie critic Jeffrey Westhoff.

For Jolie, the most disappointing failure was *Beyond Borders*, which was released in 2003. In the film, Jolie played Sarah Jordan, an upper-class socialite who becomes a UNHCR worker. In the field, her character witnesses horrible atrocities and falls in love with a doctor who has devoted his life to helping refugees. Jolie felt the film, which in many ways echoed her own life, was important because it realistically depicted the refugee situation in other countries. The film's lack of success saddened but did not surprise Jolie, who knew that the true-to-life poverty and violence shown in the film, as well as the unhappy ending, was not what most people want to see when they go to the movies.

Jolie had a different attitude about the second *Tomb Raider* movie, *Lara Croft, Tomb Raider: The Cradle of Life*, for which she was paid $12 million to once again play the cool and curvy title character. Jolie did not let the fact that the $90 million movie was panned by critics and generated only $65 million in revenues bother her. She was happy with her work and liked the movie better than the first one. She blamed the poor numbers on the timing of the release, which coincided with that of several other big-budget adventure films in July 2003.

Jolie also filmed the romantic comedy *Life or Something Like It* and the violent crime-drama *Taking Lives*, both of which were disappointments. Despite her run of failed movies, however, Jolie continued to be one of the most well-paid and sought-after stars in Hollywood. Although she could command starring roles that would pay her $10 million or more, Jolie decided instead to take smaller parts in order to devote more time to her son.

Jolie mixed real life and movies by portraying a UN refugee worker in **Beyond Borders.**

Learning to Fly

On Maddox's second birthday, Angelina Jolie promised her airplane-crazy son that she would learn to fly. By the time he had turned three, Jolie had earned her pilot's license and bought a plane.

Although she was busy, Jolie took flying classes in between her movie shoots and humanitarian work. Jolie enjoyed the challenge of learning something new, and she loves flying. Even though Jolie is known for taking risks, she has said that she is more careful about flying than anything else in her life. Eventually, Jolie hopes to donate her services to help people, possibly flying sick people to hospitals or delivering food and medical supplies to remote locations.

Movies for the Younger Set

Jolie told reporter Paul Fischer that motherhood had an influence on her decision to make the kid-friendly movies *Shark Tale* and *Sky Captain and the World of Tomorrow*, both of which were released in the fall of 2004. Even though she had only supporting roles in these films, she still found them challenging because both required her to do things in ways she had not done them before.

Shark Tale was Jolie's first animated film. In it, Jolie provides the voice for a sexy fish named Lola. Jolie tells about the first time she saw her character:

> When I was invited in to meet with them on *Shark Tale*, they brought me into this room and there were all these different pictures of fish. They were going to explain to me what they wanted me to do and I kind of looked around . . . then I saw this fish with this big red mouth and pointy eyebrows and I thought, "They can talk as long as they want. I know that I'm that fish." That was my fish. So I saw her immediately and I

knew it and I like her. It was me just kind of filling those shoes because they made her very sparkly and sexy.[69]

Jolie had fun making the movie. She could come to work in her pajamas and did not have to wear makeup. At first, she tried various voices and accents, but then the director explained that the reason he wanted her to play Lola was because he liked her voice. Jolie was flattered, since she does not like the sound of her own voice. She was pleased to have made a movie her son could see and was sure that he would like her character, even though she was the "bad" fish.

Jolie's next movie was also a new experience, because it was the first full-length movie to be shot completely on a blue screen. This meant that the actors worked on a soundstage in front of a huge blue screen with very few props. All of the background and a fair amount of the action was generated on computers and filled in later. This presented some interesting challenges for Jolie and the other actors, who had to rely on their imaginations a great deal.

At first, working with the blue screen was a struggle for Jolie, but then she began to realize that what she loved about acting was that it allowed her to try new things and take chances. Jolie talks about what it was like to shoot a scene that, when completed, would show her in the cockpit of an airplane:

> I was just sitting on this cardboard box pretending that I was sitting on something completely different. At first it felt very silly and then I think that it's great to get back to what's fun about this business. It's creative and you try things that aren't safe, get to be silly again and be bold with your choices, which was nice and refreshing.[70]

Another Mother

Jolie's next film, Oliver Stone's *Alexander*, was not for children, but as a mother, she identified with the role. In the movie, Jolie plays Queen Olympias, Alexander's devoted mother. "Olympias was smart and ambitious, and she poured all her energy into her

Jolie rediscovered the fun of acting while shooting Sky Captain and the World of Tomorrow.

son," said Jolie. "In some ways, it was a lot about survival. If I were alive at that time, I would have been a very similar type of woman, I think!"[71]

Jolie met with several challenges in playing the part. The character herself was complicated and required her to be sure everything, from her accent to the way she walked, was flawlessly executed. Jolie also found working with renowned director Oliver Stone to be both demanding and rewarding. Stone required total commitment from the actors on his set. He worked them hard and did not tolerate laziness or a relaxed atmosphere. When Jolie had ideas for her character, Stone made her back them up with reasons why the changes would be beneficial.

In addition, the part required that Jolie work with live snakes—lots of them. Queen Olympias worshipped the god Dionysus, and snakes were an important part of her spiritual beliefs. In almost all of her scenes, Jolie handles at least one live snake, and sometimes several. The snakes were well fed, but not defanged. Jolie spent a great deal of time just getting used to them. "I'd spend a lot of days just walking around Pinewood studios with snakes attached to me, trying to get them, so I could have that comfort that she [Olympias] has,"[72] she said. Jolie enjoyed working on the film, but the results were disappointing. The critics panned the movie, and it did not do nearly as well at the box office as anticipated. Once again, Jolie had chosen a losing project.

Mr. Pitt

Unlike so many of her other movies, Jolie's next film, the action–romantic comedy *Mr. and Mrs. Smith*, was a hit. Jolie earned $10 million to play a lead role opposite Brad Pitt. Jolie and Pitt play a bored couple whose marriage heats up when they discover that they are both undercover assassins, working for competing agencies.

Jolie and Pitt worked extremely well together, a fact that was noticed by everyone from the cast members on the set to the critics who reviewed the movie. "Their onscreen chemistry is 100 percent them," commented director Doug Liman, who added that "the sparks were evident from the first day of shooting."[73] Jolie and Pitt's abundant on-screen chemistry was gossiped about in the tabloids, along with speculation that their mutual attraction extended beyond the set. At that time, Pitt was married to actress Jennifer Aniston. The couple was adored by the public, and their marriage was considered to be the ideal Hollywood match. The possibility that it could be destroyed by Pitt's attraction to Jolie thrilled scandal-hungry reporters and angered fans.

And the Winner Is . . .

Angelina Jolie has won many awards, not all of them for acting and not all of them good. Some of these include:

• In 2002, Jolie was nominated to win a Blimp, the Kids' Choice Award for Best Female Action Hero, for Lara Croft, but she did not win.

• Jolie has been nominated for several Teen Choice Awards and won three for her work in *Mr. and Mrs. Smith.*

• Jolie has been nominated for four years in a row to receive a Razzie—an award that is given for worst performances of the year. She has yet to win.

• Jolie was voted the celebrity most American men would choose for a New Year's Eve date in 2003 in a survey by Blockbuster.

• Jolie has made *People* magazine's Most Beautiful People list for four years in a row. In 2005, she was named the Most Beautiful Woman. In 2006, she took the number one spot as the Most Beautiful Person. In the article, it said that Jolie's beauty was at its height when she was in the field working with refugees, sans makeup and sexy clothing.

Jolie and Pitt were rarely left alone by the paparazzi, who did their best to find evidence that the two were having an affair. Although they were occasionally seen together, no one was able to prove that they were anything more than friends. Jolie and Pitt both denied the accusations. Jolie said several times that she would not be attracted to a man who would cheat on his wife and that she would not respect herself if she became involved in such a relationship. "To be intimate with a married man, when my own father cheated on my mother is not something I could forgive," said Jolie. "I could not, *could not* look at myself in the morning if I did that."[74]

The rumors increased in January 2005 when Pitt and Aniston separated. Jolie was doing humanitarian work in Niger at the time, which made it easier for her to ignore the media frenzy. Both Jolie and Pitt continued to deny that they were anything more than friends, but the press was relentless, casting Jolie as the other woman and a home wrecker.

Speculation hit a fevered pitch in April when *Us Weekly* magazine paid half a million dollars for pictures of Jolie and Pitt in Africa. The pictures showed them walking along a beach and making sand castles with Maddox. There were no pictures of the two being affectionate toward each other, but *Us Weekly* claimed that workers at the resort said the two appeared to be in love. Jolie and Pitt, however, again denied that they were romantically involved. In addition, both Jolie and Pitt required reporters to sign a contract agreeing not to ask any questions about the rumored relationship before they would agree to do promotional interviews for *Mr. and Mrs. Smith*.

A Sister for Maddox

In July 2005, Jolie and Pitt traveled to Ethiopia, where Jolie adopted a six-month-old baby girl whom she named Zahara Marley. Zahara was in an orphanage because her mother had died from AIDS and the identity of her father was unknown. Zahara did not have AIDS, but she was ill. Within hours of arriving in New York with her new daughter, Jolie realized that something was wrong. She took Zahara to a doctor, who immediately admitted the child to the hospital. Zahara was dehydrated and had a serious bacterial infection that is common in underdeveloped countries.

After being treated with fluids and antibiotics, Zahara improved rapidly, and she was released a week later. Zahara's physician, Dr. Jane Aronson, told *People* magazine that Jolie did not leave Zahara for more than a few hours during the entire week. Jolie also made sure that Maddox was informed about his sister's treatment, explaining things to him so he would not be afraid. After Zahara was discharged from the hospital, the trio hopped on a plane to Malibu, California, to visit Pitt, who was recovering from a bout of viral meningitis.

All in the Family

During the summer of 2005, Pitt's and Jolie's comments about their relationship started to change. Rather than denying that they were a couple, the two carefully sidestepped the questions, neither

This humble building is the Ethiopian adoption agency through which Jolie adopted Zahara.

Many people speculated that Angelina and Brad Pitt, shown in a scene from Mr. and Mrs. Smith, *became romantically involved while filming the movie.*

denying nor confirming their involvement. "People want an answer about what's happening in my life and my family, but I need to know what's happening first," Jolie explains. "And I don't plan to discuss it before then. It's not about censoring myself. It's that there's nothing to say until I know that there's something to say."[75]

In August 2005, Aniston and Pitt signed dissolution papers, citing irreconcilable differences, and their divorce became final on October 2. Jolie and Pitt were seen together in public more often as Pitt joined Jolie on several of her humanitarian missions. In January 2006, they admitted to what had become undeniably obvious: Jolie was pregnant. The two still did not comment on the status of their relationship, but the pregnancy was enough to make them a couple in the eyes of the public. In addition, Pitt legally adopted Maddox and Zahara, whose last names were changed from Jolie to Jolie-Pitt. For the next few months, the family was seen in places all over the globe, including Japan, Dominican Republic, and France.

For awhile, it looked as though they would remain in France for the baby's birth, but in April the family rented all fourteen of the rooms in the luxury Burning Shores Resort in Namibia. Jolie's daughter, Shiloh Nouvel, was born on May 27, 2006. Rather than releasing Shiloh's much-anticipated first baby pictures to the public, Pitt and Jolie sold them to the highest bidder. *People* magazine paid $4 million for exclusive rights to the pictures, which appeared in the June 19 issue. Jolie and Pitt pledged to donate the money to charity.

What the Future Holds

With a new baby and plans to adopt more in the future, Jolie wants to devote as much time as she can to her family. She also

Pitt and Jolie—Two of a Kind

Angelina Jolie and her partner, Brad Pitt, have several things in common. Both have a desire to help people. Besides accompanying Jolie on some of her humanitarian missions, Pitt has been involved in UNICEF and in the ONE campaign, which works to fight AIDS and extreme poverty. He used his celebrity status to make people aware of disease and poverty in Africa even before he knew Jolie. In addition, both are considered to be two of the sexiest and most attractive people alive. They consistently make *People* magazine's annual list of beautiful people. In 2006, they were featured together with their children as the most beautiful family.

The Shiloh Nouvel Jolie Pitt wax figures debut at Madame Tussaud's Wax Museum in New York City on July 26, 2006.

plans to stay active in her humanitarian work. Jolie has recently worked to help make people aware of the situation in Darfur, Sudan, where four hundred thousand people have been killed by their own government. She has also been working to help fund education in underdeveloped countries. Jolie believes strongly that education is a right of all children, no matter where they live, and is concerned that children in poor countries, especially girls, often do not get even the most basic instruction. In addition, she recently became a model and spokeswoman for St. John apparel. Not only will she represent the company, but she will also help run a charity that the company created to fund various children's causes.

Although Jolie has stated that she would like to devote all her time to her family and humanitarian work, it does not appear that she will stop making movies anytime soon. She filmed two movies in the last part of 2005, *The Good Shepherd* with Robert DeNiro and Matt Damon, and *Beowulf*, an animated film in which she provides the voice of the mother of one of the main characters.

Angelina Jolie's life so far has been one of adventure, passion, and transformation. In just ten short years, Jolie went from being Hollywood's bad girl to becoming a devoted mother and active advocate for refugees around the world. Jolie has been asked many times if she has any regrets about her past, and she always says no: "I don't believe in regrets. I'd do everything in my life again exactly as I did it, because it got me to where I'm at."[76]

Introduction: Exceptional Angelina

1. Quoted in Trish Deitsch Rohrer, "Two Flew over the Cuckoo's Nest," *Premiere*, October 1999, p. 85.

Chapter 1: Wild Child

2. Quoted in Deanna Kizis, "Truth and Consequences," *Harper's Bazaar*, November, 1999, p. 180.
3. Quoted in Christine Blosdale, "Angelina Jolie," BeatBoxBetty. com. www.beatboxbetty.com/celebetty/angelinajolie/angelina jolie/angelinajolie.htm.
4. Quoted in Mike Sager, "Sexiest Woman Alive," *Esquire*, November 2004, p. 129.
5. Quoted in Todd Gold, "Her Jamie," *Us Weekly*, April 17, 2000, p. 51.
6. Quoted in Mim Udovitch, "The Devil in Miss Jolie," *Rolling Stone*, August 1999, p. 68.
7. Quoted in Gold, "Her Jamie," p. 51.
8. Quoted in Udovitch, "The Devil in Miss Jolie," p. 68.
9. Mim Udovitch, "The Devil in Miss Jolie," p. 69.
10. Quoted in Peter M. Stevenson, "Venus Rising," *Mirabella*, January 1999, p. 74.
11. Quoted in Chris Heath, "Blood Sugar Sex Magic," *Rolling Stone*, July 2001, p. 78.
12. Quoted in Heath, "Blood Sugar Sex Magic," p. 78.

Chapter 2: Success . . . and Sadness

13. Quoted in Michael Clark, "Angelina Jolie: The Well-Rounded Interview," Well-Rounded.com. www.well-rounded.com/mov ies/reviews/jolie_intv.html.
14. Quoted in Heath, "Blood Sugar Sex Magic," p. 78.
15. Quoted in Caroline Westbrook, "Jonny Lee Miller and Angelina Jolie . . . the Happy Couple," *Empire*, June 1996.

16. Quoted in Michael Angeli, "Tres Jolie," *Movieline*, March 1999, p. 86.
17. Quoted in Jon Voight, "Devilish Angelina—Interview with Movie Actress Angelina Jolie," *Interview*, June 1997, p. 78.
18. Quoted in Stevenson, "Venus Rising," p. 77.
19. Quoted in Elizabeth Snead, "Gia Taps Angelina Jolie's Wild Side," *USA Today*, January 29, 1998, p. 3D.
20. Quoted in Rebecca Mead, "Roles of a Lifetime," *Allure*, March 2001, p. 213.
21. Quoted in Udovitch, "The Devil in Miss Jolie," p. 131.
22. Quoted in Veronica Mixon, "Angelina Jolie Q & A," *E! Online*, November 2, 1999. www.eonline.com/Celebs/Qa/Jolie.
23. Quoted in Mixon, "Angelina Jolie Q & A."
24. Quoted in Paul Fischer, "Breaking the Rules," Cranky Critic.com. www.crankycritic.com/qa/pf_articles/angelina jolie.html.
25. Quoted in "Angelina Says Divorcing Jonny Was 'Dumb,'" Ananova.com. www.ananova.com/goingout/story/sm_874927. html?menu=.

Chapter 3: The Next Big Thing

26. Roger Ebert, "Playing by Heart," Rogerebert.com. http://rogerebert.suntimes.com/app/pbcs.dll/article?AID=/19990122/REVIEWS/901220304/1023.
27. Quoted in Angeli, "Tres Jolie," p. 51.
28. Quoted in James Kaplan, "Holy Moly, It's Angelina Jolie," *Allure*, March 1999, p. 195.
29. Quoted in Heath, "Blood Sugar Sex Magic," p. 75.
30. Quoted in *Marie Claire*, "Celebrity Profile: Angelina Jolie," February 2000.
31. Quoted in Fischer, "Breaking the Rules."
32. Quoted in Kizis, "Truth and Consequences," p. 181.
33. Quoted in Rohrer, "Two Flew over the Cuckoo's Nest," p. 81.
34. Quoted in *Marie Claire*, "Celebrity Profile: Angelina Jolie."
35. Quoted in Rohrer, "Two Flew over the Cuckoo's Nest," p. 82.
36. Quoted in Rohrer, "Two Flew over the Cuckoo's Nest," p. 81.
37. Quoted in Heath, "Blood Sugar Sex Magic," p. 75.

38. Quoted in Kizis, "Truth and Consequences," p. 181.
39. Quoted in Angelina Jolie Community, "Oscars Speech 2000 (*Girl, Interrupted*)." www.joliecommunity.com/aj_awards.
40. Quoted in Lawrence Grobel, "The Joy of Being Jolie," *Movieline*, June 2001, p. 91.
41. Quoted in Chris Connelly, "Angelina in Love," *Talk*, June/July 2000, p. 83.

Chapter 4: Love and Lara

42. Quoted in Stephanie Mansfield, "I'm Appreciating Life . . . Seeing the Possibilities," *USA Weekend Online*. www.usaweekend.com/00_issues/000611/000611jolie.html.
43. Quoted in Connelly, "Angelina in Love," p. 137.
44. Quoted in Chris Schlegel, "Q & A with Angelina Jolie," *E! Online*, June 12, 2001. www.eonline.com/Celebs/Qa/Jolie2001.
45. Quoted in Christine Blosdale, "Celebetty: Angelina Jolie (aka Mrs. Billy Bob Thornton)," BeatBoxBetty.com. www.beatboxbetty.com/celebetty/angelinajolie/angelinajolie2/angelinajolie2.htm.
46. Quoted in Prairie Miller, "Jolie on Filling Lara Croft's Shoes and D-Size Cups," NY Rock. www.nyrock.com/interviews/2001/jolie_int.asp.
47. Quoted in FeatsPress, "*Tomb Raider:* Interview with Angelina Jolie," Cinema.com. www.cinema.com/articles/486/tomb-raider-interview-with-angelina-jolie.phtml.
48. Quoted in FeatsPress, "*Tomb Raider:* Interview with Angelina Jolie."
49. Quoted in "Angelina Jolie and Jon Voight Interview," *Lara Croft: Tomb Raider*, DVD, (Special Collectors Edition), directed by Simon West. Los Angeles: Paramount Home Video, 2001.
50. Quoted in Paul Fischer, "Pump Action," Iofilm. www.iofilm.co.uk/feats/interviews/a/angelina_jolie.shtml.
51. Quoted in *Cinescape*, "Dark Angel," May/June 2001.
52. Quoted in Miller, "Jolie on Filling Lara Croft's Shoes and D-Size Cups."

Chapter 5: Changing Priorities

53. Quoted in Andrew Corsello, "Dark Angelina," *GQ*, March 2004, p. 210.
54. Angelina Jolie, *Notes from My Travels*. New York: Simon and Schuster, 2003, p. 3.
55. Jolie, *Notes from My Travels*, pp. 15–16.
56. Jolie, *Notes from My Travels*, p. 76.
57. Quoted in *Extra Daily News*, "Angelina Jolie," October 13, 2003. http://extratv.warnerbros.com/dailynews/extra/10_03/10_13b.html.
58. Quoted in UNHCR, "Angelina Jolie Named UNHCR Goodwill Ambassador for Refugees." www.unhcr.org/cgi-bin/texis/vtx/news/opendoc.htm?tbl=NEWS&page=home&id=3b85044b10.
59. Quoted in Sara Davidson, "Not Your Typical Hollywood Mom," *Reader's Digest*, November 2004, p. 78.
60. Quoted in Davidson, "Not Your Typical Hollywood Mom," p. 78.
61. Quoted in Chris Heath, "One Tough Mother," *Rolling Stone*, August 2003, p. 48.
62. Quoted in Chris Connelly, "Angelina Jolie Sets the Record Straight," *Marie Claire*, July 2005, p. 71.
63. Quoted in *20/20*, "Angelina Jolie Interview with Barbara Walters," July 11, 2003.
64. Quoted in "Angelina Jolie Interview," Cinemas Online. www.cinemas-online.co.uk/website/interview.phtml?uid=14.
65. Quoted in the *Sydney Morning Herald*, "Now Jolie Dumps Dad." www.smh.com.au/articles/2003/08/12/1060588362725.html?from=storyrhs.
66. Quoted in *Face* magazine, "Tattoo Love," August 2003.
67. Quoted in the *Sydney Morning Herald*, "Now Jolie Dumps Dad."

Chapter 6: A Life of Purpose

68. Jeffrey Westhoff, "*Taking Lives* (2004)," Rotten Tomatoes. www.rottentomatoes.com/click/movie-1130561/reviews.php?critic=columns&sortby=default&page=1&rid=1264458.

69. Quoted in Jeff Otto, "Interview: Angelina Jolie," IGN.com. http://filmforce.ign.com/articles/546/546860p1.html.
70. Quoted in Paul Fischer, "Angelina Heads to the Skies," *Film Monthly*. www.filmmonthly.com/Profiles/Articles/AJolieSky Captain/AJolieSkyCaptain.html.
71. Quoted in Remy Crane, "Angelina Jolie on 'Alexander,'" Cinema Confidential. http://cinecon.com/news.php?id=0411 221.
72. Quoted in Andrew Weil, "Angelina Jolie on *Alexander*," ComingSoon.net. www.comingsoon.net/news/topnews.php?id =7328.
73. Quoted in Michelle Tauber and Chris Strauss, "He Said, She Said," *People*, June 20, 2005, p. 67.
74. Quoted in Connelly, "Angelina Jolie Sets the Record Straight," p. 72.
75. Quoted in Christopher Bagley, "Domestic Bliss," Style.com. www.style.com/w/feat_story/060605/full_page.html.
76. Quoted in Joe Neumaier, "Angelina the Great," *New York Daily News*. www.nydailynews.com/front/story/255561p-218715c. html.

1975

Angelina Jolie Voight is born on June 4, 1975, in Los Angeles.

1982

Makes her movie debut in *Lookin' to Get Out* with her father, Jon Voight.

1991

Graduates from Beverly Hills High School at age sixteen and moves into her own apartment.

1993

Stars in her first major motion picture, *Cyborg 2;* the movie goes straight to video.

1995

Plays Kate "Acid Burn" Libby in *Hackers* and meets British actor Jonny Lee Miller.

1996

Marries Miller on March 28.

1997

Takes the lead role in the HBO movie *Gia;* separates from Miller and decides to attend film school at New York University.

1998

Returns to Hollywood and receives her first Golden Globe award, for her work in the TNT miniseries *George Wallace;* meets actor Billy Bob Thornton on the set of *Pushing Tin.*

1999

Divorce from Miller is final on February 3; receives a second Golden Globe Award as well as critical acclaim for her work in *Gia.*

2000

Receives her first Academy Award for her portrayal of Lisa Rowe in *Girl, Interrupted;* marries Billy Bob Thornton on May 5; films *Lara Croft: Tomb Raider.*

2001

Is invited to travel with the UNHCR to Ivory Coast, Tanzania, and Sierra Leone; is made a goodwill ambassador for the UNHCR.

2002

Adopts a seven-month-old Cambodian orphan and names him Maddox; separates from Thornton; severs ties with her father.

2003

Divorce from Thornton is final on May 27; is given the first Citizen of the World Award by the United Nations Correspondents Association.

2004

Meets actor Brad Pitt on the set of *Mr. and Mrs. Smith.*

2005

Adopts Zahara, an Ethiopian orphan; is given the UN Global Humanitarian Action Award.

2006

Admits to being pregnant; Pitt adopts both her children; is named Most Beautiful Person by *People* magazine, and her family is named Most Beautiful Family; daughter Shiloh Nouvel is born in Namibia on May 27.

For Further Reading

Books

Mary Lou Belli and Dinah Lenney, *Acting for Young Actors: The Ultimate Teen Guide*. New York: Backstage, 2006. A guide for teens that explains acting methods and how to find work.

Terri Dougherty, *Brad Pitt*. San Diego, CA: Lucent, 2001. Biography of Jolie's partner.

Angelina Jolie, *Notes from My Travels*. New York: Simon and Schuster, 2003. Collection of Jolie's journal entries from her first four trips with the UNHCR. Includes a foreword by the High Commissioner of Refugees and an insert of black-and-white photos from her missions.

Alan Jones, *Tomb Raider: The Official Film Companion*. London: Carlton, 2001. About the history and filming of the movie. Includes an entire chapter on Jolie.

Periodicals

Erin Bried, "Rebel with a Cause," *Self*, December 2003.

Mark Malloch Brown, "Heroes and Pioneers," *Time*, May 8, 2000.

Sara Davidson, "Not Your Typical Mom," *Reader's Digest*, November 2004.

Jessica Rimington, "More than Just a Tomb Raider, She's an Ambassador," *Teen Voices*, December 2004.

Michelle Tauber, Mary Green, and Julie Jordon, "World's Most Beautiful: Angelina Jolie" and "World's Most Beautiful Family," *People*, May 8, 2000.

Jon Voight, "Devilish Angelina—Interview with Movie Actress Angelina Jolie," *Interview*, June 1997.

Internet Sources

Paul Fischer, "Angelina Jolie Interview," Dark Horizons. September

8, 2004. www.darkhorizons.com/news04/skyc2.php.

Wikipedia "Angelina Jolie." http://en.wikipedia.org/wiki/Angelina
_Jolie.

Dominic Wills, "Angelina Jolie Biography," Tiscali. www.tiscali.
co.uk/entertainment/film/biographies/angelina_jolie_biog.html.

Web Sites

Angelina Jolie UNHCR Goodwill Ambassador, UNHCR
(www.unhcr.org/cgi-bin/texis/vtx/help?id=3f94ff664). UNHCR
page on Jolie includes fact sheet, articles on her fieldwork, journal entries, and pictures.

Internet Movie Database (www.imdb.com). Search for Jolie on
this movie database to find information about her and her
movies.

People.com (http://people.com). All the latest news about Jolie
and her family, as well as other celebrities.

This is Rachel Lynette's first book for Lucent Books, although she has written over a dozen other books for KidHaven Press, as well as many articles on children and family life. Rachel lives in the Seattle area in the Songaia Cohousing Community with her two children, David and Lucy, her cat Cosette, and two playful rats. In addition to writing, Rachel also teaches science to children of all ages. When she is not teaching or writing, she enjoys spending time with her family and friends, traveling, reading, drawing, and in-line skating.